The Final Hour

The JFK Jr. Tragedy

By

Albert Pecker

ISBN: 1-4107-0996-5 (e-book)
ISBN: 1-4107-0997-3 (Paperback)

Library of Congress Control Number: 2002096928

This book is printed on acid free paper.

Printed in the United States of America
Bloomington, IN

Photo: Comstock.com

1stBooks – rev. 02/14/03

TABLE OF CONTENTS

FORWARD

On July 16, 1999, at 1 p.m., J.F.K., Jr. called the F.B.O., (fixed base operator) at Essex County Airport in Caldwell, New Jersey. He requested that his Piper Saratoga II, call sign N9253N, be rolled out of its hangered location and parked. He asked that the plane be ready for him by 5 p.m.

He had planned to fly that afternoon to Martha's Vineyard, Massachusetts, with his wife and sister-in-law. His sister-in-law was to remain in Martha's Vineyard and he and his wife were to fly on to Hyannis.

The flight to Martha's Vineyard from Essex County Airport is approximately 180 nautical miles, and would take about one hour. The flight to Hyannis from Martha's Vineyard is 25 nautical miles and would take about 20 minutes. The total time involved would not exceed 1 hour and 30 minutes, so he would be at Hyannis Barnstable Airport by 7:30 p.m.

J.F.K. Jr. started taking flying lessons in October 1982. He obtained his private pilot certificate for "airplane single engine land" in April 1998. He received a "high performance airplane" sign off in his Cessna 182, (another beautiful airplane) in June 1998. His total estimated flight experience, excluding simulator time, was about 310 hours, of which 55 were at night. He now owned a slightly used piper PA-32R-301, Saratoga II; a single engine, low wing airplane with retractable landing gear. He had acquired the plane at the end of April 1999, operating as <u>Random Ventures, Inc.</u>, New York, N.Y. It was a beauty, a plane every private pilot would love to fly. J.F.K., Jr. had completed a "complex airplane" evaluation by his C.F.I., and was signed off to fly this plane in May 1999. He must have loved to fly this plane. During the period of May 1999 to July 1999 he flew with three different C.F.I.'s, logging several flights from C.D.W. (Caldwell, New Jersey) to M.V.Y. (Martha's Vineyard, Massachusetts), many of the flights being at night.

His estimated flight time in the accident airplane was about 36 hours, about 9.4 hours were at night. In the 15 months before the accident John had flown about 35 flight legs either to or from the Essex County, Teterboro, New Jersey area and the Martha's Vineyard, Hyannis Massachusetts area. He flew over 17 legs without a C.F.I. on board, including at least 5 at night. His last known flight in the accident airplane without a C.F.I. on board was May 28, 1999.

Witnesses who were at CDW, (Caldwell Airport) on the night of the accident stated that they saw the pilot and a female near the accident plane. The witnesses also reported that they saw the pilot using crutches and loading luggage into the airplane. One witness stated that he watched the pilot perform an engine run-up and then take off about 8:40 p.m. Now in my opening paragraph, I stated that J.F.K., Jr. called the F.B.O. and requested his hangered plane be rolled out at 5p.m. for an anticipated 5:30 to 6 p.m. departure, a flight to be conducted mostly in daylight. Accounts of John by one of the C.F.I.s who evaluated him were "he was methodical about his flight planning and very cautious about his aviation decision making." According to the NTSB, in the 15 months before the accident, John had flown about 35 flight legs either to or from the Essex County/Teterboro, New Jersey area and the Martha's Vineyard/ Hyannis, Massachusetts area, so he was very familiar with the quirky weather patterns in the Martha's Vineyard area. Further, he knew that he was not instrument rated and had problems with multiple tasks in instrument meteorological conditions.

So with the circumstances that evolved, all the parties arriving late because of the traffic jam on Route 80, and what was now an unplanned night flight, why did he load the aircraft and depart on a journey which he knew could be difficult to complete by himself.

Although we will never know the answer to that question, I have a special sympathy and insight for John, not just as a fellow man, saddened by the premature loss of young life, but also as a fellow pilot who has made, through ignorance, panic and bravado, many questionable flight decisions. I have never before wanted to talk about any of them, but I thought that letting people climb into the mind of a pilot might help them understand what it was like in John's plane in that final hour.

Read on, and see if the answer presents itself.

WITH SPECIAL THANKS

To my son Howard; who not only helped me, research the factual material in the book, write the book, edit the book, put together the pictures, maps and microsoft word disk, but remains a wonderful source of comfort to me in my golden years.

MY OBJECTIVE

Most people are very curious about the events that took place in the tragic death of J.F.K. Jr., his wife, and his sister in law. Questions like: How could this happen, what was John Jr. thinking, what was it like being in that situation, and what kind of piloting skills did he have, all come to mind?

The most common comment I have heard is, 'with all the modern equipment and technology at our disposal, to lose three wonderful, talented people to an accident of this nature, is horrible.'

People are most curious about the whole event, and little has been written or shown on television or movies about it.

I do not consider this unusual, as few people have had an experience of this nature, felt the emotions it would precipitate, and lived to tell about it.

My objective in these pages is to recreate to the best of my ability what John may have been thinking and feeling, and what may have happened, based on similar events that I have lived through while in the cockpit of a similar airplane. I will try, in the last chapter, to make that recreation using the factual data that is available, from reliable sources, making a minimal amount of assumptions.

I am a licensed Private Pilot Class C with some 430 hours logged to the date of this writing, and my experiences as a pilot, knowing I had to endure similar flying time and flight training should help me to recreate his feelings and experiences during his final flight. To this end I have written about the experiences that I have had to help the reader understand the mind of at least one general aviation pilot. I have spent some time flying in the area of Martha's Vineyard, Massachusetts and I am familiar with summer flying along the Southern and Northern coast of Long Island, and the Northern coast of Long Island Sound having flown and landed in various locations along his route, including East Hampton, Montauk Point, Long Island, Block Island, Rhode Island, Martha's Vineyard, Nantucket, Cape Cod, Hyannis, MA and Newport, Rhode Island.

I will also prepare a flight plan, using current navigation charts, depicting the area along his flight, and discuss all the aspects of the trip, including landing at Martha's Vineyard Airport.

I also hope in the following chapters to give the reader some insight into general aviation flying, by illustrating some of my own frightening and near fatal experiences and adventures as a private pilot.

I also feel it is important to relate the various procedures one must follow to obtain a private pilots license. This will establish how one feels upon going through the various training, required to obtain a private pilots license. Since all pilot training is basically the same, though the nuances of each individuals instruction may vary with location, weather and the differing personalities of your Certified Flight Instructor, it is likely that John Jr. went through the same process.

The pilot trainee has to pass the same rigorous training, both by enduring difficult physical flight conditions, and written testing.

Since I know nothing about J.F.K. Jr.'s relationship with his Certified Flight Instructor or his feelings or motivations, I will relate my own; I make no correlation between myself and him other than the bond of common experience.

FLYING LESSONS

I guess it was logical to wonder why someone at my stage of life would want to learn to fly. I'll try to explain.

I started taking flying lessons, (as my log book reveals) on April 4, 1978. I was 47 years of age, married, with two children. I lived in Westfield, New Jersey and worked in New York City as a Civil Engineer for the Board of Education and had started some side business ventures as a Builder/Developer,

So I had some extra dollars for flying lessons.

My marriage was not working, and I needed to keep my sanity, so I started hanging out in my spare time with a friend and a business associate Sol, who was a pilot and had his own plane, a beautiful "Piper Comanche", call sign, 2.R.T., (pronounced Two Romeo Tango). How verbally beautiful it was to me. I loved to say "Two Romeo Tango". Sol, was 10 years older than me and had started flying as a young Army Air Force Officer during World War II. He loved to relate his experiences flying a DC3 tail dragger over the hump in Burma. He was a really competent pilot, and held an I.F.R., (Instrument Flight Rating).He was also single, divorced, with two grown children.

We had some really good times together. Sol had some lady friends and he would arrange a foursome for tennis, flying, dinner, or all of the above. We would often jump into the plane and fly to Doylestown, or other town close to an airport, for a special dinner or a night out. The relationship led to my meeting another of Sol's friends, who was also a pilot. Jack was about the same age as Sol and had been a Pilot, for the Navy, in World War II. He flew some hot Navy planes and loved to talk about his carrier flying days.

Well, it was a great little group; pilots, women and mucho fun!

I thought "if these two can fly, well, I can also,", and so the adventure began! I applied for flight training at my local flight training school, located at Linden Airport, Linden, New Jersey.

Upon application, I received three things:

1. A pilot log book, to record all of my flying activities
2. An extensive flight manual with a kit to do flight planning and calculations.
3. A wonderful 1st flight with my new C.F.I., (Certified Flight Instructor)

Of these three items, the one I remember most, and got me thinking of the insanity of my decision to get my pilots license, was my first flight in this little plane.

Most flight schools train the fledgling pilot in one of two planes; a C150, or it's newer version, a C152. The C stands for Cessna. The 150 or 152 denotes it's engine horse power ratings. Both are two seaters and are mostly used as training aircraft, as they are inexpensive to purchase and cheap to operate. At first sight, the C150 and 152 are tiny, and appear almost flimsy, especially compared to the big jets that we see at commercial airports.

My first flight at flight school was very traumatic for me. I remember entering and seating myself in the C150 and immediately feeling very claustrophobic in the confined quarters of the airplane's cockpit.

My C.F.I. gave me a quick review of the maze of instruments on the control panel and showed me a check list to review prior to flight.

"Yeah, that's the Altimeter", he said "you need that to know what altitude you are flying at. Remember here at Linden Airport the big jets flying into Newark Airport make their landing approach over us and they are at 3,000 feet so we cannot fly over 800 feet. That's our traffic pattern altitude."

'Something else to worry about,' I thought.

"That's the air speed indicator, and that's the artificial horizon, and that's the turn and bank indicator and that's the gyro compass and that's the stationary compass", and on and on.

I kept thinking, "does he expect me to remember all this at this time?" Besides, is this all important; I don't know if I am going to get through this flight alive. Anyway, I decided that if I survive this flight, I'll worry about the details later.

I started the engine, after calling "Clear Prop", which I did very well, the propeller spun, and my

C.F.I. yelled "she's all yours", over the noise of the engine.

I am going to stop here because I do not want to convey to the reader that the airplanes or the C.F.I. or anything about flying or the procedures are unsafe or substandard, because they are not. Its just that, as a beginner, I did not know this, and I was scared. Well, you have to have some faith in the system, I reasoned, so I grabbed the yoke with my left hand, put my right hand on the power lever, my feet on the rudder pedals, and listened to the instructions of my C.F.I. Much to my amazement, my brain absorbed and disseminated the information given by my C.F.I., transmitted it to my arms and legs, and this little flimsy plane taxied out to the runway. I gave it power as directed, watched the air speed indicator reach 60 knots, pulled back on the yoke and within seconds we were airborne. I kept thinking, "This is great, hope my luck doesn't run out!" We climbed to 1500 feet, an altitude that is always bumpy, and flew out of Linden, New Jersey in the general direction of Solberg Airport in Readington, New Jersey. After a while we climbed from 1500 feet to 2500 feet. I felt a little better as we gained altitude.

During the flight my C.F.I. gave me some basic instruction on climbing, descending, and turns.

What scared me was when we had to cut down on the power to make our descents. What if it wouldn't power up again? I seemed to feel best when the power was on and we were climbing.

7

As we returned to Linden Airport and started our decent to landing, I was somewhat relieved. I convinced myself however, that I would not let a sense of calm set in until we were safely on the ground.

After the first experience of my first training flight, I reasoned that I would hang in with this nonsense for as long as I could and see where it takes me. I was wagering in my head that at this time, the odds of my becoming a pilot were not good.

THE FLIGHT MANUAL

My next step in learning to fly was to tackle the nasty looking flight manual. This is a big thick book with a lot of boring information inside.

I knew my training as an Engineer would help me understand the technical side of flying and subsequently master the flight manual, but getting back to the books did not particularly appeal to me. Besides, risking ones life flying is much more macho and exciting.

Flight manuals vary according to Authors, however the subject matter is basically the same. The purpose is to prepare for the Federal Aviation Regulation (F.A.R.), written quiz. The flight review book I have is composed of 16 chapters. I will give you the headings and discuss each briefly.

Summary of Flight Manual

Chapter 1: The requirements of flying as defined in Part 61 of the F.A.R.s.

Chapter 2: Basic principals of flight, how and why planes fly and the explanation of various forms used to describe flight.

Chapter 3: Various flight instruments, i.e.: Pitot Tube, Airspeed Indicator, Static Ports, Altimeter, Vertical Speed Indicator, Compass, Artificial Horizon, Gryo Compass, etc…

Chapter 4: Engines used on planes, describing the basic principals and terms of the reciprocating engine, including aviation fuels and octane ratings.

Chapter 5: Airplane weight and balance, describes how to calculate the weight of all items to be carried on board as well as the physical airplane to determine if the weight and center of gravity is with in manufactures acceptance limits for this airplane.

Chapter 6: Airplane Performance: which includes best angle of and best rate of climb, true air speed, and differing density altitudes.

Chapter 7: Airport and Airspace: Terms like controlled and uncontrolled airspace, automatic terminal information service, glide scopes, visual approach slope indicators, etc.

Chapter 8: Weather and all terms associated with weather.

Chapter 9: Weather services and how to use them.

Chapter 10: Flight information services and publication thereon.

Chapter 11: Navigation and the terms used therein. Latitudes, Longitudes, Meridians, Time Zones, and all terms used therein.

Chapter 12: Radio navigation and all terms used therein. You are required to obtain a radio operators license when taking flight lessons, as you are using the radio.

Chapter 13: Composite navigation and cross country flight training.

Chapter 14: The effects of flight on the human body and how it affects the body in different attitudes.

Chapter 15: Handling airborne emergencies, the facts that are most commonly cited in general aviation accidents. The equipment on board to use to indicate an emergency and how to use it. This is a very important chapter - it could save your life.

Chapter 16: A chapter on the various Federal Aviation Regulations pertaining to flying, including terms and definitions.

I hope the aforementioned chapters did not bore the reader, but the information contained therein is absolutely essential to the pilot in learning to fly.

My objective here was to illustrate the varied and diverse subject matter used by all pilots in performance of their duties.

Albert Pecker

LEARNING TO FLY

I bet myself that I would never learn to fly, I was convinced that I was not the pilot type. I was also unsure of this little flimsy C150 I was flying in!

Another concern were the individuals who were giving me instructions, the so called C.F.I.s. I started taking lessons with one C.F.I. and suddenly after 5 lessons he would be gone, and I would be assigned to another C.F.I.

I tried hard to assimilate the information given me and perform the flying techniques to impress my C.F.I., so I could elevate myself to the first plateau, the solo flight, but it seemed that every time I impressed my C.F.I. that I was good enough to solo, I got another C.F.I., I was getting discouraged. Each C.F.I. would be a stickler for some maneuver that I had not yet mastered to his satisfaction.

In order to solo, you have to know the principals of takeoff and landing, all types of turns and some slow flight. Stalls (Aerodynamic) are also important, especially on take offs and landings. Since stalls are important, let me try to explain what a Stall, (Aerodynamic Stall) is. A stall occurs when the lift component, that force which affords the wing lift, is gone. It happens when, on takeoff, you lift the nose too high and come in with power such that your wing's angle of attack is at an angle that the lift component is

12

gone.   The plane will then vibrate, shutter, and the nose will drop. It is important for a pilot to recognize this, so that the nose can be lowered below the horizon and stability reestablished. When lowering the nose of the plane, it is important to keep equal force on your rudder pedals to avoid a spin, which can cause the plane to go out of control.

An approach to landing stall can also occur, as power is cut or lowered when landing, and if the nose is raised too much, a stall will occur. In this case you must come in with power and again allow the nose to fall below the horizon until stability is re-established.

By the way, with regard to my flimsy C150 remarks, when I observed how the plane handles under stall conditions, steep turns, bumpy flying, and slow flying, I realized that this airplane can take a lot of punishment, and I could not believe how sturdy and strong it really was.   The airframe is composed of structural aluminum members with an aluminum skin, which is riveted to it forming a single rigid unit.

Well it finally happened.   After 11 hours of training my C.F.I. said, I was ready for my pre-solo check flight.

I was excited and happy. I could not wait to be able to take the plane when I wanted, and do take offs and landings, but my pleasure was soon shattered, when the flight school switched my flight instructor and I had to take 7 more hours of instruction before I was allowed to solo! My thoughts at the time were that it cost about $55.00 an hour to fly, and these bastards are trying to prolong this as long as possible. When I reached 18 hours of training, my C.F.I. finally released me for my solo flight.

I must admit that the solo flight is scary. No matter how ready to solo, I thought I was, I was scared. There is something about being up there, all alone, for the first time. What if I did do something wrong, or if I forgot something, there was no one there to correct me. I could faint, or panic, or anything could go wrong, and its all over. It's unbelievable how many weird thoughts went through my mind prior to my first solo flight test.

On September 20, 1978, 5 months and 16 days after my first training flight, I passed my solo flight test. I had to do take offs, and landings, for one hour, a big accomplishment for me.

Now that I had completed my solo flight, we began the next phase of my training, which was cross country flying. I had to plan and fly six cross country trips. Three trips were with my C.F.I. on board, and three were solo. At this stage in my flying career, this would not be hard, but at the time my navigation skills were nil and I had almost no training in the use of omni navigation, which was the standard radio driven navigation equipment used on most planes at the time, from my little Cessna, all the way up to the big 747's.

On top of that, all trips were to be done using 'dead reckoning' procedures. This meant studying the navigation map, and picking off landmarks and terrain features with enough precision to reach my destination, without the use of electronic navigational aids.

It is important to understand that when you are flying 2500 feet off the ground at 120 knots per hour, it is easy to miss something on the ground. The house that is so recognizable from the driveway just looks like a dot, or worse, may be completely covered by the canopy of the two nearby oak trees. We could also track using our compass but the wind will blow you off course, so you must be careful. I was fortunate enough to complete the three cross country flights with my C.F.I. onboard without incident. He was so pleased with my progress, he allowed me to proceed with my solo cross country flights.

My first cross country solo flight, the shortest of the three trips, was to Pottstown Memorial Airport, Pottstown Pennsylvania. It was a beautiful flight. There were no clouds, no bumps, just good easy flying, and I was there and back in two and a half hours.

The second Cross Country solo flight was planned to Lancaster, Pennsylvania Airport, and then return, stopping at Allentown, Bethlehem Easton Airport, and back to Linden. On November 20th, 1978, piloting my flying schools C152, call sign 7142November, I departed. The day was beautiful, but the air density was high (thin air) because the weather was hot, with a stiff cross wind, which made for bumpy, uneven flying. As I flew the plane, it gained altitude, without my adding power or elevator direction to climb. With the constant bumping I thought the airframe would crumble from the terrible shaking and bouncing. I felt something was wrong with the airplane's controls. I kept gaining altitude, uncontrollably and the cross

15

winds kept blowing me off course. To make matters worse, the navigational landmarks were terrible. I was to cross a river and three major highways and the airport was supposed to be ten minutes passed the third highway, but the bumpiness of the ride and the planes unexplained tendency to climb, made it hard to follow these references. Lancaster airport is a Class 'D', it has a control tower and a A.T.I.S.[1] but no radar. I passed the third major highway, twenty minutes went by and no Lancaster Airport in sight. I did not even see the city. The airport is supposed to be North of the city. I dialed 120.9, the control tower frequency of Lancaster into my communication radio, hoping to hear something. As fate would have it, I noticed the tail of an airplane in front of me during the majority of my flight who was flying at the same altitude as I was, but a good 5 to 10 miles away. I of course did not know the pilot's destination or purpose, but I figured that his flight might be the same as mine. I also noticed a small suburban city to my South and, as I passed it, I made a large sweeping right turn to the North looking for the airport. No airport was visible at this time however, so I resumed my Westerly course. I kept thinking, 'whatever airport I see, that's where I land. To hell with this cross country nonsense!' When I resumed my westerly track however, one thing became evident. I was gaining on the plane in front of me, as it was clearly in sight now. I was still concerned about my predicament but flying conditions had improved,

---

[1] A.T.I.S. is an automated terminal information service that can be picked up on the cockpit radio.

the bumps and thuds stopped, and the plane stabilized it was no longer gaining altitude on it's own. I had been flying for about an hour now and had 5 hours of fuel on board when I departed, so fuel was not a concern, but I was troubled by the fact that I had originally estimated the flight would take 60 minutes and nothing was in sight as I had passed my last major highway landmark some time ago and all I could see now was a vast array of small hills, valleys and lots of cultivated farmlands.

I thought of calling Lancaster control, but I did not want to admit to anyone that I was hopelessly lost. I figured, who knows, if I admit I'm lost they will fail me on this cross country flight. Then I am back to square one and I did not want to do this trip again. I did have one consolation however, the plane in front of me. I hope they are not flying to Chicago, I thought to myself to relieve the tension.

Then it happened! I heard a crackling over my radio as the plane in front of me radioed the tower.

"Lancaster control this is Charlie 6725, I am lost, I can't find the airport. I am on a cross country training flight. Please help me!"

The plane in front of me was just as lost as I was!

I'm saved, I thought, I hope the plane in front of me is making that call. I patiently waited for the reply from Lancaster control.

"Don't worry Charlie 6725, we'll find you. What is your position?" came the reply.

Albert Pecker

"I estimate, I 'm due East of the airport, don't know where", Charlie 6725 replied.

"We are sending a helicopter out to locate you Charlie 6725. Keep looking and let me know when you see him."

I started looking for the helicopter that was to save Charlie 6725. In about 5 minutes '6725', acknowledged the sighting of a helicopter, which I could see in the distance in front of me as well. Well, needless to say, I followed the helicopter, and the lost plane in front of me to the airport, landed and rolled up to the parking area.

I had to have my log book signed by the training official to acknowledge my successful flight.

"How was your flight?" the training official inquired?

"Well, it was bumpy, lots of cross wind. It took me 20 minutes longer than I had planned" I replied.

"Guy in front of you couldn't find the airport. We had to send a helicopter out to find him" he said.

"Too bad," I said, "Please sign my log book, I still have to fly to A.B.E. today."

He signed my book. I went outside and saw another pilot walking toward me.

"Just fly in" I asked.

"I flew down here from Hartford, terrible day for flying, I am an hour late, terrible cross winds. Kept

gaining altitude, bumpy ride. I am glad to be down."
came his reply.

Relieved and satisfied. Glad I am not losing it. I
boarded my little C152 and started out for A.B.E.,
(Allentown Bethlehem Eastern Airport), the second leg
of my trip. The flight back to Allentown was non
eventful and things went rather well. By the time I
spotted A.B.E., which was North of my route of flight,
I had been at this for three and a half hours; two and a
half hours of flying, and at least 1 hour at Linden
airport in preparation of the trip. There was a lot of
items to review and memorize, especially since I was
not using navigation aids, as it was a dead reckoning
flight. A.B.E. is a big sprawling airport located just
North of the center of the three cities. I had notes on
the runways at A.B.E. and the approach patterns, but I
did not know the active runway, the one in use at the
time of my arrival. I called the control tower and was
told runway 13 was in use. I entered the pattern, saw
runway 13, and started a left hand approach to landing
with clearance from the control tower. Suddenly I get
a call on my radio.

"November 7142 do not land! You are using the
wrong runway. Abort landing!"

I veered off to my right, climbed and did a go
around the airport. It appeared that the airport has a
runway 13 right and 13 left. They were using 13L for
take offs and 13R for landings. The incident left me a
little shaken. I don't know how I did it, but I landed
the plane and got the training official to sign my log

book, and returned to Linden airport. The flight back took about one hour.

This completed the 2nd of my cross country solo flights. The really long one and the last of the three series was Linden to Harrisburg, Pennsylvania then to Cape May, New Jersey, and return to Linden. I was not looking forward to this flight. Having endured much stress from my last flight, I decided not to do the third and last until I was satisfied with all my preparation procedures. I studied the terrain from Linden to Harrisburg to Cape May and to Linden again until I memorized it. I made up a sheet for each leg of the trip, showing each airport I would fly by, including each control tower call signs. I studied my emergency procedures especially radio distress 121.5, and transponder 7700. I even reviewed some navigation omni call signs in case I really got lost. When I felt confident, I called the school and booked the plane.

Since I had completed all my other cross country trips successfully, my C.F.I. had no comment to this trip. On December 5, 1978 I departed Linden airport in the flight school C150, call sign 68358, for Capital City Airport in Harrisburg, PA. This would be the longest solo flight I would take to that time with an estimated time of flight of 2 hours and 15 minutes.

The route of flight was similar to my first and second solo flights, so I kind of knew the route and the terrain to the point that my last solo flight terminated, at Lancaster. It was a good flying day so I encountered few problems with the flight.

Shortly after flying past Lancaster airport the huge Cooling Towers of 3 mile island nuclear power plant became visible. This was my navigational landmark and the entrance to Harrisburg, PA, Harrisburg International Airport, and Capital City Airport, my destination. It was truly a beautiful sight. I gasped as I flew by just to the North of this magnificent complex.

The flight to Capital City took 2 hours and 10 minutes. I had my book signed, I refueled and was airborne in 30 minutes. So far so good I thought, but, knowing me, I figured something unexpected will happen. It always does!

The flight to Cape May was quicker than I thought it would be. I headed East back towards Lancaster airport, Southeast to New Castle County airport, Southeast to Millville and continued Southeast to Cape May. The sights were beautiful and the total flight time was 1 hour 36 minutes. Per the procedure, I had my flight book signed, had a cup of coffee and started my return flight to Linden. I was feeling pretty good, and my confidence level was high. All went well until I reached McGuire Air Force Base airspace.

I was flying just off the shore line about 2500 feet enjoying the sights when, out of the blue, I hear a crackling sound and a super sonic boom! In front of me, not very far away and crossing my flight path was a jet fighter plane rising from left to right. At this point I did not know what to do. In collision avoidance I would turn to my right but the jet plane was going so fast that whatever I did would not help much. I decided to stay on course. I did not know if any more occurrences were forthcoming. I dialed McGuire on my radio and transmitted my position and established radar contact. Soon thereafter and again without warning another jet crossed my flight path and then another. I must be doing something wrong I thought, but McGuire control said nothing. I continued flying on course and within 25 minutes I had Linden airport in sight.

"Well, this phase of my training is complete", I thought. "And I am still alive!"

At the time I finished my cross-country flights I had 42 flying hours logged in my book. In the months that followed my successful cross-country flights, my flying lessons at Linden airport with the Linden C.F.I.s went nowhere. It seemed like we kept repeating the same maneuvers over and over again. My friend Jack, who belonged to the Sky-Hi Flying Club in Manville, New Jersey, (Now known as the Central Jersey Regional Airport), suggested that I join his flying club. Then some of the club members could give me flying lessons. I had logged at this time 57 hours at Linden flight school and no talk of a release in sight for a flight test. In desperation I joined Sky-Hi flying club and started taking lessons from one of the club members who held a C.F.I. license. Within 2 months and 20 hours of flying time I was released for a final flight test. I took and passed my final flight tests on July 30, 1979.

FIRST FLIGHT AFTER LICENSE

When you first get your pilots license and you realize you can take people flying, it's a great feeling.

You absolutely rack your brain trying to figure out whom you will ask, and give the honor of flying with you. So on August 7, 1979, 8 days after taking my flight test, I set out to fly my C150, (belonging to the Sky-Hi Flying Club, of which I am now a member) from Kupper Field in Manville, New Jersey to Zahn's Field in Farmingdale, Long Island. You know upon looking back on this, I was really a gutsy guy. Gutsy probably defined here as stupid. Two factors drove me to perform this feat:

1. My fly buddy, Sol, always poked fun at guys who got their ticket (a term us fly-boys used when someone got their license), and never flew anywhere except in the pattern at their local airport. I vowed not to be one of them.

2. Upon receiving my ticket, I wanted to impress my sister with what a great brother she had, so I called her and set up to meet at Zahn's.

My sister was married and had 2 children; they lived in Oceanside, Long Island. Zahn's was at the time, a convenient place to meet, and a 15-minute drive for my sister and a one-hour flight for me. It was a beautiful flight to take, very picturesque, awesome sights. The flight was as follows: Kupper, Manville, NJ east towards Linden Airport, Linden, NJ, (it's good sense when flying to navigate airport to airport in case of mechanical problems), East over Staten Island, NY, to the Verrazano Bridge, with a spectacular view of New York Harbor, looking south, and the Statue of Liberty looking north. Continue east along the Atlantic shoreline passing Coney Island, Riis Park and the Rockaways. Within 10 nautical miles of J.F.K. international airport you are required to call Kennedy control to notify them that you are flying within their airspace.

All of this was very exciting to me. There I was in my little C150, all by myself, flying over the New York shoreline, talking to Kennedy control, like a real pilot! Most controllers are very nice, accommodating and helpful. I guess it depends on what kind of day they are having, but being up there all by yourself in this little plane, looking at this vast expanse of sky and sea, I really didn't care what kind of day the controller was having. When flying in the vicinity of J.F.K. international airport the regulations are 500 feet along the shoreline or above 7000 feet.

Well, I was not about to climb out to 7000 feet above the airport, so I elected to go down to 500 feet and fly along the shoreline.

Upon calling Kennedy control the controller informed me that if I elected, I could fly directly over the airport if I stayed at 1500 feet.

I was a little nervous about this, but I thought it such a thrill that I graciously accepted and started to climb up to 1500 feet. At 1500 feet, I turned and started my course over the direct center of J.F.K. international. The flight over J.F.K. was approximately 25 or 30 nautical miles and should take about 15 minutes at most. It just seemed that I was moving very slowly, what was a 15-minute fly over, felt like an eternity. I kept thinking, the controller was nice enough to let me fly over and he must think I'm jerking around moving so slow. I looked at my airspeed indicator, it read 110 knots. Why am I moving so slowly? It was getting me nuts! I figured I must have been running into headwinds, that's why I am not moving. It seemed like I was standing still. I must have seen 20 take offs and landings of big jets passing under me during that fly over. After a while I passed the center of the airport. Heaven bless me I thought, it wouldn't be long now.

My course took me back out to the Atlantic shoreline and I flew east towards the Jones Beach monument. At Jones Beach monument I altered my course from east bound to north bound and Zahn's airport could be seen clearly about 5 miles away.

Zahn's was a one-runway strip about 3000 feet long. The runway ran north - South, it was typical of another era when we had small airports with single strip runways. Well, the excitement grew as I called Unicom and requested the active runway. It was a beautiful day, a few small clouds, bright blue sky, and unlimited visibility.

Albert Pecker

I landed without incident, parked the plane and started looking for my sister, who I knew would be anxiously awaiting to honor and congratulate her brother. Well, I checked the parking lot, looked in the few buildings open there and could not locate my sister. I knew this was Zahn's airport, it showed Zahn's on my New York sectional aeronautical chart, but I was not sure my sister knew where it was. I located a phone and called her but there was no answer. After about 15 minutes I noticed my sister's car drive into the parking lot and park. My sister of course, did not show, (beauty parlor appointment), but my brother in law and my nephew were there with smiling faces. We had a great afternoon, my nephew Todd and I flew out over Jones Beach and Oceanside Bay to look at his house from the air. Then we returned to Zahn's and my brother in law Danny and I repeated the first flight. They were delighted, both flights were flawless and my confidence was building by the minute. I was however anxious to return, as I had a long flight back and it was getting late. I wanted to avoid any change in the weather and I was not up for night flying at this time.

Upon our return to Zahn's, I told Danny and Todd it was great for me to take them flying and we would do it again soon. I carefully preflighted the C150 again, refueled to insure I would not run out of fuel, and took off. This time I decided to decline any offers from J.F.K. control and fly at 500 feet along the coastline. After leaving J.F.K. control I climbed out to 1500 feet and continued across New York Harbor, across Staten Island direct to Kupper airport.

The sights were magnificent. Too bad this is not a four-seater, like the C172. Then I could have taken Danny and Todd together in one trip I thought to myself. I returned to Kupper, landed safely and vowed to get a check out flight in the C172 owned by the club. I locked and tied down the plane, completed my logbook and set out for my drive home. Not bad I thought to myself. I might get to be a good pilot yet!

My confidence was definitely building.

Albert Pecker

FLIGHT FRENZY

My married life during the period I was learning to fly was not good. While marriage to my first wife was never the best. It was now very bad. I had moved out of the house on several occasions only to reconcile and move back in. I was now however convinced that my children would be fine and that my current marriage would never work out. With this in mind, I subsequently fixed up an efficiency apartment in one of the small apartment houses I had built, and irrevocably moved.

On August 16, 1979, 9 days after completing my historic flight to Zahn's to be honored by my sister, I was getting a check out flight in the Ski-Hi Club C172, a four-seater. Let me at this juncture explain; an individual can get his pilot's license to fly and he can fly the plane he got his license with. To fly another type plane, a pilot must get a check ride with a licensed C.F.I. All planes are basically the same but there are differences, so it makes sense that check out rides are required. I had previously described the C150 as being small, a two-seater. Well, as I sat in the C172 with a C.F.I. on my right, the passenger seat, and looked out on my left and right side at the wing span of this plane, I was amazed. The wingspan seemed enormous compared to the C150, it's little brother. The interiors of both planes are basically the same with regard to the control panel. All instrumentation is the same and except for the size of cockpit, wingspan, engine, etc. it's basically the same. The C172 is more powerful having 170 horsepower engine vs. 150 Horsepower in the C150. It also has more wing surface so it lifts a little sooner and goes a little faster.

My checkout flight ride went well and 90 minutes later I was legally able to pilot a C172. Well, that was it, not only could I fly the C150 but now I could also fly the C172. No one was safe! No matter whom I spoke to, associated with, business or socially, a fly with me invitation was forthcoming. I flew Jack, my aircraft carrier navy pilot buddy, my lady friends, their lady friends, my banker, my lawyer, more lady friends, my real estate broker and so on. In fact word of my flying prowess grew so rapidly in my family, my sister requested that I return to Zahn's, and she was there this time, actually waiting for me. She even had my brother in laws brother Jimmy with her so I could take him for a fly. This was the big time for me.

A SWEET HEART OF A DAY

I am sure that the reader knows that I am really poking fun at myself in these descriptions so I'll get a little serious at this point. My son at the time I moved out was 22 years old and attending Lehigh University, and my daughter was 16 years old, lived at home, and was in Westfield High School. I don't know how I did it, but I convinced my son Howard to fly with me.

My army air force buddy Sol, always described a great day as follows, you fly into this little airport on Montauk Point, Long Island. The airport is at the very tip or end of the island, near a beautiful old light house.

When you land at the airport ask the owner, he has an old fire truck and will drive you out to the end of the island where you can use the beach. Talk about quaint, picturesque and beautiful! Who could ask for more. I convinced Howard that this would be a great way to spend the day So on September 16, 1979 my lady friend Linda and I departed from Kupper airport and flew to Zahn's airport to pick up my son and his girl friend Ellen. Ellen lived on Long Island in the vicinity of Zahn's and also attended Leigh University. Howard was visiting her at the time.

Linda was kind enough to prepare a picnic lunch and everyone brought a beach blanket.

The day was beautiful, the flight was flawless, and Montauk Point airport and its surrounds were exactly as Sol had described it. We landed and were driven by the fire truck to the beach and spent a wonderful afternoon relaxing on the sand by the sea. Very few people were there, the only way to get there was by air via the airport or by dune buggy. We started our flight back by 4:30 p.m.

As I previously stated I would find Zahn's by referencing the Jones Beach monument and coursing north. I was lazy by not taking an intersecting omni for a cross reading, but I flew visually and the monument was very prominent.

As fate would have it a ground fog rolled in, in the unpredictable weather patterns of the area and the monument could not be seen from the air. Proper flight preparation is always necessary when flying. You can not stop for help and errors are compounded when any confusion sets in.

We actually flew past the monument and the point where I alter my course northbound. Now I had flown into Zahn's on several occasions to visit my sister and this morning and I thought I was familiar with the area. Lucky for us all my son, Howard, who is very bright was able to pick a cross heading off the sectional aeronautical chart, while in flight, which we dialed into our navigational omni. Using the cross bearings we turned, headed north and found Zahn's. I of course felt bad, as P.I.C. I should have planned the flight better. You can not depend on visual reference no matter how familiar you are with an area. We

31

landed safely at Zahn's, the kids debarked and thanked us for a great day. Linda and I flew back to Kupper and landed without incident.

No one said a word about my little navigational mishap, but I felt bad. Howard never flew with me again. It is now 23 years later and I am still flying.

THE BIG MEETING

With all this flying and good times it was only logical that something would come along to squelch it. I met the love of my life and current wife, Enid.

During the period one receives flight training and prior to being released for your test flight with a F.A.A. examiner, you practice many flight maneuvers over and over again.

These include:

1. Takeoff and landings
2. Flying straight and level
3. Medium turns and steep turns
4. Climbing turns
5. Descending turns
6. Stall[*] recognition and recovery
7. Slow flight in all configurations
8. Soft field takeoffs
9. Short field takeoffs
10. Cross wind takeoffs and landings
11. Flying under the hood[**]
12. Turns around a point

---

[*] Stall here defined as aerodynamic, not engine stall.

[**] The hood is a device you wear on your head which allows you to view the instrument panel only and not look outside.

Now I might be missing some maneuvers, but you get the idea. The one series of maneuvers, most disturbing to me was flying under the hood. This is of course necessary if one finds themselves in a situation where visual flight is impossible, visibility is zero.

A private pilot, one not instrument flight rated (IFR), is required to have certain flight visibility minimums before attempting to fly. This is called a V.F.R. flight, visual flight rules, in effect.

The minimums are; for controlled airspace:

1. Surface to 10,000 feet you must have3 miles visibility
2. You must stay 500 feet below clouds and 1000 feet above.
3. 2000 feet horizontal clearance from your plane to a cloud

Getting back to flying under the hood; most maneuvers while flying under the hood are not bad, if one remembers not to look outside and trust the instruments and observe what they are telling you, i.e. the artificial horizon, air speed indicator, vertical velocity indicator and your altimeter.

By observing all the instruments and using your brain you won't get too disorientated. Under calm conditions with your C.F.I. sitting alongside, using instruments is not to bad. The portion which is difficult is when you are training under the hood and the C.F.I.

puts the plane in an unusual attitude and says, "you recover".

. Well I always automatically put both feet on the rudders and equalized them to avoid a spin. Then I quickly observe the airspeed indicator, if my airspeed is increasing, (I am in a dive) so I cut or come back on power, if my airspeed was decreasing, (I am climbing) so I add some power. Then I quickly observed my vertical velocity indicator to confirm the above. Well this all sounds easy and uncomplicated, so I suggest you try it sometime! Anyway you have to be able to do this to get your license. I set my brain to think about it and burned it into my memory.

To return to our events, the flying euphoria continued. Everyone I met was invited to fly. I met Enid October 30, 1979 at a singles dance. She was divorced, the mother of two boys, Bruce age 13 and Fred age 11. As a second date, I invited Enid to go flying with me.

On November 18, 1979 we were in the C150 flying to Blairstown, New Jersey airport. I liked to fly to Blairstown it is up in the mountains of Sussex County, New Jersey. The airport is a single strip field with a cute restaurant that made the best soup, french fries and homemade apple pie. Within walking distance of the field was a small lake, which was part of a swim club. No one was ever there and we would come and go and use it whenever we flew to Blairstown, and many is the time we would skinny dip, if we had the right women.

Wow, if Enid was nervous about her first flight with me, she did not show it. Girl friends never complain much about anything, but when you marry that's another story! Well I was acting my usual gay, debonair pilot type, talking and laughing, we were having nice conversation over the noise of the engine.

By the way, I always carefully preflight the plane, and did the check list with anyone I took flying. I always explain my every detail and every flight maneuver. I knew this inspired confidence with my passengers in my flying ability. I never forgot my first flight and how scared I was.

Well this being our first flying date, I was busy impressing and I liked this lady, so in the heat of the moment I lost count of mountain ranges. Without thinking, I said, "I believe Blairstown should be right here, I must have lost count of the mountain ranges".

Well instant panic set in, all of my inspiring talk and procedures were quickly dismissed by Enid. She was quiet for a minute, while I calmly said, "It must be over the next mountain range", but when it didn't appear the verbiage began. I don't recall all that was said, but the phrase "Get me safely down and you can have anything you want" sticks in my head.

What happened? Navigation equipment changes as the years go by. When I first started flying we used omni station navigation. This is basically a radio signal emanating from strategically placed stations. We had two navigation radios on board and by crossing or intersecting two radio beams we found our geographic locations. I usually flew on the one beam until I crossed another and then I knew where I was. There was one good radio beam at Blairstown coming from Solberg V.O.R., the cross beam from Sparta V.O.R., never somehow came in at Blairstown. I guess the hills and mountains blocked it.

Now I flew into Blairstown a lot so I stayed on the Solberg V.O.R. northbound to Blairstown and didn't bother with the Sparta cross beam. I knew when I flew over the fourth mountain range, Blairstown airport would emerge. Well, naturally, silence prevailed until the next mountain range, upon which Blairstown Municipal airport miraculously appeared in the distance.

Enid and I, upon arrival at Blairstown, had a great time. Everything went well after the navigation mishap. No skinny-dipping though. I did, however remembered her "anything you want" remark. I figured I'd use it at an opportune time. Well we had several fly dates after that, none of which evoked any mishaps.

Our relationship grew and we decided to take a fly vacation to visit my mother in Fort Lauderdale, Florida.

Albert Pecker

OUR HONEYMOON VACATION

On December 27, 1979 Enid and I boarded the C172, call sign 7106G, and departed for Fort Lauderdale, Florida, to visit my mother. We thought it would be a great vacation for many reasons.

I wanted to introduce Enid to my mother, even though I was still married to my first wife. I hadn't seen my mother for a long while, and Florida in December was usually nice and warm, and I wanted the flying experience.

I had flown down to Florida with Sol in his Piper Comanche, 2RT, four years earlier and I did not anticipate any problems. Enid had to be back to work on January 2, 1980, so we had six days to complete the vacation. I figured a day to fly down, four days in Florida and one day to fly back.

I did a lot of trip planning for this flight. I got a trip ticket from A.O.P.A., (Airline Owners and Pilots Association) which looks similar to AAA or Allstate Motor Club, except it shows air routes. I studied all the sectional maps and did flight calculations, the whole works. It was a tight trip, time wise, I had to have good weather and since I did not know the areas it had to be daylight flying.

Enid had a good job, since her divorce she had to support herself, her two boys and her household. So getting back on January 2nd was important to her. I

38

planned to be at the airport by 6 a.m. and depart by 7 a.m. and fly for 12 hours or at least till dark.

Well, we did not get to the airport until 8:30. We did not lift off until 9:00. 3hours en route, Enid had to go to the bathroom! We landed at the next airport en route which was Norfolk, Virginia. There we made a pit-stop, refueled and was back in the air in 45 minutes. By the time we were airborne it was obvious that it would take 2 days of flying to get to Florida. With six days to spend, 4 days of flying was not practical. So clear heads prevailed, we changed our vacation plans and headed for Hilton Head, South Carolina.

We arrived at the airport in Hilton Head at 4pm.
We were both happy about this; Hilton Head was a beautiful spot. We found a Ramada Inn on the beach, we rented bicycles, we went out to great dinners, it was a real honeymoon.

Now, there is an interesting twist to this story.

The night before we were going to depart we were getting dressed in our hotel room prior to dinner, and the TV. was on. The program coincidentally was about instrument flying. They were stressing the fact that under poor conditions, and bad visibility, the pilot must rely on his instruments and discount all of his personal feelings as to his attitude. Most of all, they stressed, do not look out the window. Enid was glued to the TV., I was rather casual, saying that I knew all that.

Since Enid had to be back at work on January 2nd I thought it would be best that we leave on the 31st of December, maybe spend a night in Atlantic City and fly home on the 1st.

We arrived at Hilton Head airport at about 8:30 a.m. for our flight back. I checked the weather, it was marginal V.F.R., but improving. Enid was reluctant to go, she said she concentrated on the marginal portion and I on the improving portion. Anyway, I said we will try it, if it gets bad we will turn around, do a 180, and come back.

We packed the plane, I did my preflight inspection, refueled and took off. It seemed I had visual when we flew at about 1500 feet, above that it looked very cloudy. I stayed at 1500 feet for about 30 minutes and suddenly we were completely engulfed in clouds. Zero visibility, we could not see anything. The propeller was not visible, nor were the wing tips. I thought about turning around but I was so panicked, and so busy watching the deteriorating weather and just flying the plane, that I didn't know which way to turn.

Pure panic set in, I did not even have the good sense to have called a flight service station to establish radio communication.

Enid was frantic, she started raving, "I was crazy to take this trip" Suddenly she stopped, "listen to me" she said, "I watched the program last night, keep your eyes on the instruments, don't look outside, just watch the instruments!" I told myself, 'fly this plane, remember under the hood.' Air speed increasing, cut power your diving, air speed decreasing, come in with power.

As soon as I noticed that we were completely engulfed with clouds and I had lost tracking or navigation I dialed 121.5 on my communication radio and tried to call someone. I heard nothing. At the same time I dialed 7700 on my transponder, which constitutes a mayday, loss of communication, navigation, etc. I heard nothing.

I flew the plane for what seemed like an eternity not knowing where I was or where I was going. I tried to head westerly, knowing that the Atlantic Ocean was in an easterly direction, but the storm just kept blowing us in an easterly track. In the next 30 minutes I must have pulled power 20 times and come in with power 20 times. I could swear I was looking down into water more than once. I vowed to fight on and never give up. I knew we had plenty of fuel on board, so I could go on.

Enid repeated over and over, "Keep your eyes on the instruments, don't look out!"

Just short of what seemed like forever, a voice broke through on the radio. I will remember that voice and what he said for as long as I live.

"This is the Coast Guard, low level radar station off Myrtle Beach, South Carolina. We have been trying to reach you for an hour now. We have you on our radar screen, we know your position. You are at 1500 feet and 25 miles out over the Atlantic. Do not panic, we have you. I have 2 helicopters warming up in case you go down. We could be there in 5 minutes. Do you read me?"

I picked up the mic' and replied, "yes I read you."

His voice came back, "Listen to me, do not panic. I want you to climb up to 2500 feet and come to a heading of 270 degrees. I will take you into Myrtle Beach, South Carolina on a precision radar approach."

It seemed like a weight was lifted from my head and shoulders. Un-afraid, un-panicked, unaware of my precarious position, I eased back on the yoke, came in with power and climbed to 2500 feet, upon reaching 2500 feet, I altered my heading to 270 degrees and waited for further instructions.

Within minutes the clouds seemed to dissipate and we were looking at the landing approach runway in Myrtle Beach, South Carolina.

I thanked our Coast Guard savior for his help, he saved our lives and put our plane down amongst all the big jets at the airport.

Enid declared that she "was not getting back on this plane. We are taking a commercial flight home!"

I said, "look, let's go into the airport and get a cup of coffee, we'll talk about it."

My knees buckled as I departed the cabin and my feet touched the ground.

We had our coffee (coffee never tasted so good), the weather cleared, the sun shone, and we boarded our little C172 that stood, so piteously, among the big jets.

We flew to Norfolk airport, Virginia, where we stopped on the way down. We took a motel close to the airport and spent New Years Eve at a local Chinese Restaurant. The next day we flew into Bader Airport in Atlantic City, New Jersey walked the boardwalk, had lunch and flew back to Kupper airport in Manville, New Jersey, our point of origin.

In all of my years of flying I always kept an accurate account of all my flight activities, but I was so embarrassed over this incident that I could not bring myself to record it in my log book. I did learn an important lesson; never fly in marginal weather, and if in trouble turn around immediately.

I was never a macho pilot after this incident, I was just happy to be alive!

SUMMER FUN, SUN, AND SPATIAL DISORIENTATION

Enid and I were a couple now. I kept the efficiency apartment in Linden, but I kind of moved in with Enid. 'Kind of', here, means not officially.

Enid lived in a one family, colonial house in Edison, New Jersey with her two sons. There was no major conflict between me and the boys. They did their thing and I did mine and all went well. Enid worked as a sales person in classified advertising, she had little time for household chores, so we had someone come everyday who cleaned and cooked. It worked out well for all of us.

The flying incident at Hilton Head left a scar on both Enid's and my mind, but we both never discuss it much.

The flying frenzy continued, only now we were flying Enid's friends and business associates as well as my friends. We flew Saturdays and Sundays of almost every weekend. We liked to fly to Block Island. The flight took a little over 1 ½ hours. Once we arrived we would take a taxi to town and walk around enjoying the sights. Sometimes we rented bicycles or scooters and rode around the island. We always ended up at Ballards. The food was good, the band always sounded the same and we would use the beach and shower facilities.

We would depart for home about 4:30 - 5:00 p.m. so we could refuel at East Hampton airport and be home by 6:00 - 6:30 p.m. at the latest. It was a great time and flying made it better.

Weather conditions were the prime factor in all planning of flights, if the weather was not good, we did not fly. The trip over water from Montauk Point to Block Island could not be more than 20 miles, yet I always dialed in and communicated with a flight service station for sound watch over water.

Weather conditions for summer flying were tricky, you could have a sunny day but poor horizontal visibility due to smog and haze. Yet vertical visibility was good, you could look up and see a sunny sky.

During the best times we would have three planes visiting Block Island for the day. Jack flew one, Sol flew one, and I flew one. One couple Enid and I planned some summer fun with was Lee and Joan. Both Lee and Joan were divorced, they were not living together but spent a lot of time together.

On July 19, 1980 the four of us boarded 34832, a beautiful C177 RG, the top plane owned by the Ski-High flying club, and we departed for a fun vacation.

I had checked out on the C177 RG with one of the C.F.I.s who belonged to the Sky-High flying club in December 1979, when the plane was first acquired by the club. The C177 RG, (RG stands for retractable gear) this was the most update, sophisticated plane I have had the pleasure of flying. It had a constant speed, variable pitch propeller and when it's landing

45

gear was retracted, it could cruise at 140 knots, at least 20 knots faster than the fixed landing gear planes I had been flying. I was never too happy with this airplane, however because the landing gear set up looked rather inferior.

C.F.I.s are a pain in the behind; well, not all of them.

My Biannual flight review was due in May 1980. Amazingly enough it had been 2 years since I received my license. Now, I knew how to fly the 177 RG, I had passed the qualifying flight in December 1979, and had flown it several times with no incidents.

While taking my biannual review with one of the club's C.F.I.s, who by the way did all of my qualifying flights, he suddenly felt I should have more time and instruction in this airplane. He passed me on my renewal flight review, but suggested we schedule more time on the 177 RG. ·

On a subsequent lesson after I had taken off with this plane about 50 times with no incident he decides I am not pulling the landing gear retracting lever properly on take off, so as I take off this one time and pull the landing gear lever, the gear starts to retract, and he suddenly pushes it down and then up again. Well, you can't do that! You must wait for the gear to be fully up or down, full cycle, before pushing the lever. Realizing that the landing gear is now stuck in the middle he said, "Don't worry there is an emergency pump here, I'll pump it down!"

He pumps, I pump, meanwhile I have to fly this airplane. Nothing happens. We decide to fly around the airport while he pumps the emergency pump. We also call the unicom, at our airport to tell them we believe our landing gear is stuck, because we can't see anything and have no indication it has gone down and locked into position.

They call the fire department, his wife, my Enid, and send another plane to fly along side us to see if the gear is down and locked. The other pilot says "It is not locked down."

My C.F.I. gets the brilliant idea to climb to 5000 feet and do power dives so the gear will come down by itself with the G force. We did power dives for one hour. It's a good thing I had nothing to eat prior to flying! Finally, the pilot flying nearby says, "I think the gear is down".

By this time every fire truck in Somerset County is at the airport, the police, the newspapers and the mayor. They were about to foam the runway. My C.F.I. also got the brilliant idea that we should fly for four more hours to use up the fuel on board.

My brilliant idea was to land at a nearby seaplane field in Old Bridge, New Jersey. They told us to keep away. They wanted none of us.

Well, the big moment came. My C.F.I. had his shinning moment, he took the controls and showed me how to do a slow, soft field landing. Through some miracle the landing gear held and we landed safely.

All this because he was refining how I moved the landing gear lever up and down.

Getting back to our vacation with Lee and Joan. We planned to spend 3 days in Nantucket, 2 days in Cape Cod and 4 days in Newport. We had a weight limitation as to baggage so the women had to rough it. We had to fly to Blairstown, New Jersey first for the mechanic to check something on the airplane before we could begin our trip. It was a lousy way to start a vacation but I had no choice. We were all in good spirits so there was no problem and Lee was always an up-guy and made the best of all situations.

We departed Blairstown at 11 a.m. and reached Nantucket by 1:30. The trip took 2 ½ hours. Not bad for Nantucket. We parked at the airport and took a cab to town and our bed and breakfast.

A small room awaited us with no air conditioning but who cared, we were in Nantucket and on vacation! We had a really good time, going to the beach, long walks, sight seeing, good seafood, great weather.

On the fourth day we arrived at the airport around noon. Loaded the plane, preflighted and took off. Our destination was Provincetown, Massachusetts. It was a bright sunny day, beautiful blue sky and blue water. We departed in a southerly direction, flying right into a sunny blue sky.

The flight over water across the sound to Provincetown on Cape Cod was about 30 nautical miles. Provincetown is due north of Nantucket. Total distance to Provincetown is 60 nautical miles, and

48

estimate flight time was 45 minutes. I climbed to about 1500 feet in a southerly direction and began 180 degree turn north towards Cape Cod, in a nose up attitude. I remember looking down to look at the airport in a nose up attitude, looking at the blue sky and sea ahead of me and I felt queasy. Everything started to spin, I lost concentration, my subconscious said turn around and land.

I felt secure in that we could not be more than seconds out over the entrance to Long Island Sound with land just behind us. As I pushed forward on the yoke the plane leveled off and I felt better. No one in the plane knew I had a problem. The whole incident probably lasted 30 seconds.

I could not believe the feeling I just experienced, it came out of the blue. I stopped looking outside and concentrated on my flight instruments. I felt this was the way to over come this experience of spatial disorientation.

The flight took longer than I thought, the airport was difficult to find on a sea of sandy beaches. What I planned as a 45 minute flight took one hour. After landing and securing the airplane we took a taxi to our motel.

We did not like the area, we didn't like our motel so we spent the night and the next day we started out for Newport, Rhode Island. Enroute to Newport the weather got rainy and some fog set in, so we landed at Barnstable airport in Hyannis and spent the night at a motel near the airport.

The next day when we awoke the sun was shinning and within 2 hours we packed, boarded the airplane and arrived at Newport State airport. We were ready to enjoy ourselves and the sights of beautiful Newport.

We spent a relaxing, truly wonderful 4 days at Newport. We rented bicycles and rode around visiting the mansions and enjoying the sights of the town. We ate at nice seafood restaurants and strolled along the streets for our evening exercise. We could not use the beach as the red tide was in. On the 5th day we awoke and took a taxi to the airport.

I preflighted the plane and we departed climbing up to 4500 feet. I pointed the nose towards Kupper and we were home within 48 minutes, for a beautiful flight, with the plane handling flawlessly. Everyone was very happy and pleased.

Sadly enough it would be the last time I was to fly 34832. Four days later one of my co-members in the Sky-High flying club was flying in the vicinity of Millville airport in New Jersey and crashed the plane in a landing attempt.

A LITTLE SOUTH HAMPTON BEACH, A LOT OF STUPIDITY, AND A LITTLE LUCK

It was July 1981, my divorce from my first wife was almost complete, it was almost 2 years since the action was first instituted. Enid and I were living together now for about two years, unmarried.

Our adventures in flying continued unabated. An acquaintance of mine who had a travel business in the same building I had my office in expressed a desire to fly. Since Enid and I liked to make new friends we planned flying dates with Judy and Howard. One weekend we flew to Danbury, Connecticut. Another weekend we flew to Trenton - Mercer Airport, Trenton, New Jersey.

Trenton - Mercer was a nice size airport at the time and had a policy where they allowed commercial flights and private pilot flights to park at the same terminal building and use the same facilities, so it was cool to fly in, park, and we use the restaurant.

One Sunday, the last in August of 1981, the four of us flew in and sat down for a casual lunch. I had received a weather briefing the evening before and the morning of this flight. It was for favorable conditions throughout the day with no mention of thunder storms. As fate would have it, while we were having lunch the sky blackened and a horrific thunder storm erupted. It lasted about 20 minutes, the rain then stopped, but the dark clouds did not move on.

We finished our lunch and waited about 45 minutes for the skies to clear, but it just remained overcast with pockets of clearing.

Now I knew that we could not just sit there all afternoon so I had to make a decision, do we chance flying back to Kupper in Manville, New Jersey or rent a car and drive back.

Well since Hilton Head I vowed no more stupid stunts. So we rented a car and drove back to Kupper airport. I was very proud of myself in exercising good judgment, even though one hour later the skies cleared and the rest of the day was beautiful. The next day I drove the rental car back to Trenton - Mercer and flew the plane back to Kupper. I was a little miffed at the extra effort of this experience, but I theorized that this was all part of flying.

Shortly thereafter Enid received a call from her cousin Barbara inviting us out to their house in East Hampton to spend the day with them. Barbara had told us of their house in East Hampton and extended an invitation many times but we always had other plans. On this occasion the timing was perfect and since we had flown into East Hampton airport, Long Island many times we graciously accepted the invitation. At Barbara's insistence to bring friends we invited Judy and Howard and they accepted.

The plan was to spend some time at the beach and go back to their house for a barbecue and then fly home.

On occasions like this, where I have to fly, and spend time at the beach, and then fly home, I'm always a little tense for two reasons, one being the weather, the other being if I spend too much time in the sun I get a headache. Since I had to pilot back to Kupper I would never drink alcohol or stress myself out.

The day of the flight the weather report read like a broken record for the area, visibility 3 to 5 miles in haze. The weather report was bad, but we met the minimum requirements, so off we went. In a phone call, prior to departure Judy said that Howard had some prior commitment, but that she would love to come along.

We met at Kupper and flew direct to East Hampton, the weather was scruddy, low visibility, haze, mist, etc., but the minimums held. We arrived safely, a bumpy but otherwise comfortable flight.

Barbara and Lloyd were wonderful hosts, we parked the plane, boarded their car and were off.

We stopped at the sub shoppe and got some delicious looking subs, soda, etc. and set out for South Hampton beach with all our belongings.

After parking at the beach parking lot we trudged along the beach for what seemed like miles to find this very special section of South Hampton Beach that Barbara and Lloyd called "their spot". Upon finding this sacred ground, we set up our chairs, blanket and supplies and settled in for a fun time, but when I fly, I can't relax. I was always watching weather patterns and the sky. The haze was getting worse and the visibility was decreasing. The visibility at our sacred ground though was definitely improving.

Upon settling in Barbara asked if we would mind if she removed the top of her 2-piece bathing suit. Before the vote was in she shocked us by just pulling off her top and to second the motion Lloyd declared he needed some air and removed his bathing trunks. To our surprise, Judy said "You guys should have told me, I would have worn a 2-piece suit!"

Barbara solved the problem by suggesting to Judy, "Take it all off!" Which she promptly did. I did not want to be a poor sport, so I joined in by removing my swim trunks. Enid was the only one who did not undress, she simply busied herself by taking snap shots of the rest of us.

It was a great day for the beach, the haze kept the sun from getting through. There was a nice breeze and the water was warm to bath in. Once everyone removed their bathing suits, (except Enid) we all became close friends and we joked and laughed. It was obvious why we had to walk so far to get to this portion of the beach; it was the so called "nude section".

Despite the distraction, I couldn't completely relax, as I was concerned about our return trip. I would have preferred to fly back in daylight. Another concern was that we had no headlight in the airplane, it had burnt out. So illuminating the runway at night was out. I knew this as it was noted by a previous club member when he last used the airplane. It hadn't concerned me at first thought, as I was not planning to do any night flying on this trip.

As we finished our pleasant day at the beach, our host insisted that we come back to their house.

They had planned a steak barbecue for this evening. We were having so much fun, that I decided to stow my concerns, seize the moment, and have a good time. Besides the weather was deteriorating fast. It looked like rain for sure. It was near 6 p.m. when we left the beach and started for Barbara and Lloyd's house.

By 8 p.m. we had all showered and were seated for a delicious steak barbecue. While we were having dinner rain and thunder broke loose. It lasted about 2 hours. I was getting very antsy, I felt I would like to return the plane tonight, it was a flying club plane. I did not know who had it booked for tomorrow. At 11 p.m. I went outside, the skies looked clear. I called the weather, they said improving conditions, some low clouds.

"Well," I said "Let's go".

I devised this plan, since I had no working headlight on the plane, we boarded the plane and I taxied out to the runway with Lloyd right behind me with his headlights on to illuminate the runway. I cautioned Lloyd that I may have to stop the plane at some point and he should be ready to stop suddenly. I felt at some point that I must be crazy to attempt this but what the hell, a challenge is a challenge. Judy and Enid hated the plan but they went along anyway.

Well, it all worked out okay. I taxied to the active runway did my run-up and lifted off, of course Lloyd was behind me all the way to give me light. I had an eerie feeling about all of this as the airport was completely closed down, no lights, no activity, no people, just us.

Pretty good plan I thought to myself as we lifted off and I did a right down wind turn to a westerly heading. Then my stupidity came into play. I looked down to see the field I had just left, it was gone, all I saw was darkness, black, nothing at all. I looked west, saw some clouds, some haze. I thought to myself, "what if the weather report was wrong?" There was no field down there to land on. I said nothing of course, my only hope was to call ahead to JFK control and have them take me in on a precision radar approach. That would be assuming that the weather patterns ahead were not good.

As I proceeded westbound the skies cleared and we flew along very nicely. I called JFK control and they gave me clearance to fly through. I didn't even have to alter my course. We were safely back at Kupper airport by 2 a.m. The flight time was 1 hour 45 minutes.

Remember the little luck? We all need it sometime. I later found out that if I dialed the East Hampton unicom number into my radio and clicked the mic' 5 times all the lights on the air field would come on.

Talk about stupid.

Albert Pecker

COW PASTURES CAN BE DANGEROUS

Looking for new places to fly to was always a very pleasant task. Some pilots even publish a news letter with locations they flew to and the activities one could participate in once they are there.

Enid and I were still together, our relationship was going well. I had kind of settled in her house and in spite of small differences things were good for both of us. I was finally officially divorced from my first wife after two years of prolonged court proceedings. We still flew every weekend with various friends, but now we became very friendly with Enid's "Edison friends".

As is usually the case, many of your friends talk about going flying with you but only a couple will actually go through with it.

I still worked for the New York City Board of Education as an engineer and commuted into the city every day. I also still did building and development work as a side venture and had my office in Linden, New Jersey. For some reason, I guess it was more convenient, I decided to join the Rari-Ten Flying Club in Linden and give up my membership in the Sky High Club at Kupper airport in Manville, New Jersey.

The Rari-Ten club had only one plane while Sky High had 2 planes but Rari-Ten had only eight active members to Sky High's fifteen members. The Rari-Ten club plane was a piper Cherokee (P180), a low wing beauty. It was a kick to fly a low wing plane after always flying a high wing Cessna. On December 21, 1982, my 51st birthday, I officially checked out on 5367 Foxtrot a piper Cherokee, P180.

Naturally everyone I knew and who wanted to fly was invited to fly my newly acquired happening. One couple from our Edison friends really liked to fly with us. Stan and Rosalie were always up for a fly. We flew to republic in Beth Page, Long Island and had lunch at a model 87th fighter squadron restaurant on the field. We flew to Caldwell, New Jersey and had lunch at a similar restaurant. We flew to Allaire in Wall Township, New Jersey to have lunch in their quaint restaurant.

It sounds like we ate a lot but the scenery on these bright, sunny day flights was spectacular, and flying was serene and calming. It made for a good time and *mucho* comradary.

One flight we decided to take on October 20, 1986 was to Rhinebeck, New York. We heard that they put on a spectacular air show at this field. It featured original planes from WWI, (World War I). Bi-planes, Tri-planes, some running on kerosene, some with the entire engine rotating with the propeller. I was told you could fly into the field and park and watch the show "for free". So, being the idiot I am I decided to do so. I did exercise a note of caution on the flight to Rhinebeck, New York, (which field lies just east of the Hudson River). I radioed a nearby air field and inquired as to the possibility of a direct fly in to old Rhinebeck field. Duchess County control advised that old Rhinebeck field was an old cow pasture and advised landing at Sky Park airport and taking a taxi to the show at old Rhinebeck.

As is usual for me I thought, hell with this, by the time I land at Sky Park, taxi to old Rhinebeck, half the show will be over with. I'll land at Rhinebeck, if all those other planes can land so can I. Well, we flew direct to Rhinebeck, I did a circle around the field, called the Unicom and landed. We parked the plane and made our way to the stands which lined the air field and runway on the Western side. The runway not being clearly defined, was in fact a bumpy old cow pasture.

We seated ourselves and watched a truly magnificent air show. It was daring flying stunts of all kinds spins, loops, figure eights, the whole works. The show combined flying stunts with various vignettes and stories centered around WWI, with the Red Baron and Blue Max. The Tri-planes and the Bi-planes landed and took off with ease, bouncing along the cow pasture field and lifting off or landing.

The show ended about 4:30 - 5:00 p.m. We waited for the crowded stands to empty somewhat and the four of us made our way back to the 5367 Foxtrot. I preflighted the plane as was my normal custom, checking fuel, oil and all systems. We boarded and secured our seat belts. I taxied, did a run up, looked for a wind sox and started down the pasture into the wind.

Much to my surprise the maximum speed indicated on my air speed indicator as we bounced down the field was about 45 knots. Now I need 60 knots to pull up the nose for take off.

I became a little panicky as I aborted the takeoff roll and turned around to taxi back to my starting point.

I thought those old planes took off and landed all day with no problem, but they did not have four people on board and with all the wing area they had, they only needed about 40 knots to get a lift off. Well my challenge was at hand, I had to get this plane out of here. I will have to do a bad terrain soggy field take off I thought to myself. Of course I had not done this since flight training and then there was only two of us on board and the other guy was my C.F.I. I also remembered I wasn't too good at this maneuver. Well, I wasn't going to drop Rosalie and Stan here, so here goes! I guess those guys still left in the stands will really see a show now, I thought to myself.

I poised at the beginning of my takeoff run, came in with full power, pulled the yoke back hard as we began rolling. As the plane lifted off the ground slowly I flew along the ground until I had some 60 knots on my air speed indicator and lifted the nose to climb out.

In front of me was the tall trees that stood at the north end of the field. I'll never make this I thought, as we lifted higher and higher and I can't abort this take off now. As we rose into the tall trees I noticed to my right a small separation between two of the trees.

61

Thinking my landing gear which was not retractable will surely hit the tree tops. I veered over to my right. As we flew I kept waiting for an awful crunching sound. As luck would have it we cleared the trees and climbed unscathed by this adventuresome event. It's funny, Stan, Rosalie and Enid were talking so much they never knew about what they just went through.

Of course, I never mentioned the event or what took place, until now.

A SAD DAY FOR FLYING

It was almost five years since I first met Enid and we began living together. Sol, my flying buddy and mentor, who introduced me to flying and single life, and Jack who rounded out our trio of pilots, were still seeing their lady friends, but no move-ins; I was the solo dissenter.

Sol often cautioned me about my move - live in, especially with a women who had her two children living with her. He predicted an eventual break up with lots of grief. In fact, Sol and Jack thought seriously about my removal from our exclusive single pilots club, it was only because we all had so much fun together that they included Enid and I.

Enid's boys, Bruce and Freddy and I somehow managed to get along together. I was busy working most of the time as was Enid. We had a housekeeper who cleaned and cooked for us, so the house was always clean and there was always prepared food for dinner. The boys were very resourceful, they ate when they were hungry and usually cleaned up after themselves. They also had their friends and their school work to occupy them, so things kind of worked out for all of us.

The year was 1984, Bruce, Enid's oldest turned 18 and went off to Ithaca College. Naturally Enid and I decided to fly up to Ithaca to visit Bruce. This was

63

kind of a new experience for me as I had never flown in this area of the country before. I studied the flight charts, checked my navigation procedures, studied the location of the O.M.I. stations and felt fairly confident that it would be a successful flight.

In those days we did not have global positioning stations (G.P.S.), for navigation we flew with vector omni radio (V.O.R.), signals for directional navigation. I planned the trip so that I would fly from airport to airport. The V.O.R. stations that we flew to were usually located at an airport, so this worked out well.

Basically I planned the route of flight as follows:

1. Linden airport to Solberg airport in New Jersey
2. Solberg airport to Scranton airport in Pennsylvania
3. Scranton airport to Binghamton airport in New York
4. Binghamton airport to Tompkins County airport in New York

Tompkins County airport is close to Ithaca and Bruce was to meet us and pick us up at the airport.

But this was a different kind of flight than what I was used to because I would have to fly at higher altitudes. Pilots flying visual flight rules (V.F.R.) when flying over 3000 feet above ground level fly at assigned altitudes depending on the direction of flight. Zero degrees to 180 degrees fly at odd thousand plus 500 feet, 180 degrees to 360 degrees fly at even thousands plus 500 feet. These altitude differences are designed for collision avoidance. In the direction we were flying our assigned altitudes would be even thousands plus 500. So I would have to fly, when over 3000 feet, 4500, 6500 or 8500 feet altitudes. Now I usually fly at 2000 feet to 3000 feet altitudes. I kind of like to see the ground terrain and what is down there. Also I can identify ground objects to check on my on board navigation. On short flights, which I usually take this works out well. On long flights, flying at higher altitudes is usually more efficient, as fuel consumption is lessened due to thinner air. On this flight to Ithaca we had to pass over some mountain ranges with obstructions to 3100 feet, so I had to plan to fly at 4500 feet from the Delaware Water Gap mountain ranges on to Binghamton.

The date was September 16, 1984, we arrived in Linden airport at 10 a.m., we boarded our P180, 5367 Foxtrot and we set out for Ithaca College in New York State. It was a beautiful day for flying; blue sky, bright sunshine, little white puffy clouds, cool temperatures, a day that makes you happy you can be up there flying around. I love to take a deep breathe and let the air out slowly, it felt so good being up there flying on a day like this.

The flight from Linden airport to Scranton went real well. We started flying at 2500 feet and climbed to 4500 feet as we came into the higher mountain ranges. While flying at the higher altitudes around the Scranton Pennsylvania area I noticed the clouds were getting thicker and more plentiful. On V.F.R. flights we are required to maintain cloud clearance as follows: Between 1200 feet and 10000 above surface…within controlled airspace:…500 feet below clouds…1000 feet above clouds…2000 feet horizontally. Prior to the clouds becoming thicker and more plentiful I was able to maintain my cloud clearances without too much trouble. Remember I had to fly at 4500 feet, so go tell the clouds not to be at 4500 feet! At this point I decided to climb to 6500 feet as I would be on top of the cloud layer. Once at 6500 feet everything was clear and unobstructed.

Remember, I had no traffic advisories and was not in communication with anyone. I had not filed a flight plan and flying around these clouds made me nervous as I could not easily spot another aircraft. I continued flying at 6500 feet when I noticed the clouds beneath me were getting solid, no breaks, like before. Also I knew Binghamton V.O.R. (airport) was getting close, only 20 miles out. It was important for me to identify Binghamton to check on my navigation and position. Well, "this is it", I thought to myself, I have to get down! I told Enid about our predicament and advised that she hold onto her seat as when I do see a break in the clouds below we will fly or dive down through it.

Well, eventually there was a break in the clouds and John Wayne or Tyronne Powers would be proud of me as I maneuvered and dove down into the open space. It turned out that the visibility below the clouds at 2500 feet was excellent. We were right on course as we flew over Binghamton V.O.R. station to Tompkins

County airport. The total trip took one hour and forty five minutes.

We met Bruce, toured Ithaca College, had lunch and departed for home.

To fly home we climbed up to 5500 feet, it was exactly 5:30 p.m. eastern standard time when we departed Tompkins County airport. The skies were clear. The return flight was flawless. At exactly 6:30 p.m. we sighted Linden airport and landed. We tied down our P180, 5367 Foxtrot and were home relaxing in front of the television by 7:00 p.m.

What a great day we had. Up to Ithaca and back, we left at 10 a.m. and returned at 6:30 p.m. On the news that evening they announced a plane had crashed in Linden. The crash occurred at 6:45 p.m., about 15 minutes after we landed at Linden airport that evening.

The next day I learned that the pilot and one of his sons were killed in the crash and three more people were seriously injured, one of them was the pilot's other son. The second son died a few days later. I had flown with Steve, the pilot who crashed. We were both members of the Sky High Flying club at Kupper in Manville, New Jersey. Steve had a C.F.I. rating. He and my Buddy Jack were good friends. Coincidentally his wife and Enid worked together at what was known then as the National Telephone Directory.

THE FINAL HOUR

The NTSB report of John Jr.'s final flight is quoted extensively throughout the rest of this text. It can be found on the NTSP web site, and is public information, in the public domain.

I plan to present the final chapter as follows:

1. How I would plan and fly the trip from Essex County airport, Caldwell, New Jersey, (symbol C.D.W.) to Martha's Vineyard airport, Vineyard Haven, Massachusetts, (symbol M.V.Y.).

2. How J.F.K., Jr. flew the trip as narrated in the N.T.S.B., (The report is part of public record.) and my personal analysis of the event based on the N.T.S.B. published report.

3. A copy of the N.T.S.B. report as I received it on the internet.

I hope that the material presented here aids the reader in gaining a better insight to this tragic event and aviation in general.

MY FLIGHT PLAN

In order to have a successful flight we have to plan it properly, we want no surprises, and we want to anticipate the unexpected or eliminate it.

Most important on the evening before and the day of flight, get an up to date weather briefing.

Next, by using our New York sectional navigational chart to plan our route of flight. It is important that the chart be up to date, preferably the latest edition.

For John Jr.'s flight, I'll list the navigational waypoints:

1st leg - Essex County, (C.D.W.), direct to Sikorsky Memorial,
    (B.D.R.).

2nd leg - Sikorsky Memorial direct to Groton, New London
    (G.O.N.).

3rd leg - Groton, New London direct to Martha's Vineyard,
    (M.V.Y.).

Albert Pecker

It is important that we have information along route of flight in case of a problem we can contact the closest airport enroute for emergency landing, or navigational aid.

Airspace is also important. We must determine who's airspace we are flying in and contact the proper control tower for collision avoidance control.

Caldwell - Essex County - C.D.W., C.T. 126.5 Control Tower
A.T.I.S. 135.5 - Air Traffic Information Service
G.R. 122.95 Ground Control

Essex County is situated in New York T.C.A., (traffic control area).

Therefore, upon takeoff you cannot fly between altitudes of 3000 and 7000 feet and you must contact 118.3, (E.W.R.) Newark control to notify them you are flying in their, (N.Y. T.C.A.) airspace.

Before taking off we will adjust our radio and navigational units by dialing in the proper call signs, the ones we will be using on active and the secondary numbers on stand by.

On our *Garmin* G.P.S. we will dial our first leg destination which is B.D.R. for Bridgeport. Once activated the G.P.S. unit will give us our position and all other information we need to navigate the 1st leg of our flight.

When we contact Newark control it is possible that they will give us radar traffic advisories while we are in their airspace with a hand over to LaGuardia control. If this happens we will not have to contact Teterboro, (T.E.B.) and Westchester County, (H.P.N.) airports.

Since we will be flying by Teterboro, (T.E.B.) we will also call Teterboro control at 119.5 to inform them of our position.

We will also fly by Westchester County, (H.P.N.) airport control tower 118.5, we will also call to inform them of our position.

The next radio communication will be with Sikorsky Memorial, (B.D.R.) control tower 120.9 to notify them of our intent to fly over in their airspace.

We will do this when we are within 10 N.M. of their airspace.

Once we pass Westchester County we can begin to climb from 2500 feet to 5500 feet altitude.

If we have LaGuardia control they will give us clearance for this.

We will also have to estimate that this 1st leg of our flight, which is roughly 60 N.M., it should take us

about 30 minutes. So a check on the time is important upon reaching Sikorsky,
(B.D.R.).

Upon leaving B.D.R. airspace we will change our course heading, and fly direct to Groton, New London, (G.O.N.).

We will dial KGON into our G.P.S. and press enter, enter, etc.

The course now will be 90 degrees, the nautical miles about 50, our time in flight 25 minutes.

At this point I will call New Haven airport, (H.V.N.) control tower, 124.8 and tell them I am passing thru their airspace.

Within 10 nautical miles of G.O.N., I will call the control tower and tell them I am flying in their airspace.

Upon reaching G.O.N. I will set my G.P.S. Global Positioning Unit to KMVY and press enter, enter and alter my course to 100 degrees direct to Martha's Vineyard.

The flight distance is approximately 74 nautical miles and should take about 40 minutes.

I want radio contact with my flight over water so I will dial my F.S.S., (flight service station) at 122.1 for sound watch, or if I can not make contact I will call M.V.Y. control at 121.4.

While calling F.S.S. at 122.1 or M.V.Y. control at 121.4, I will also request an updated weather briefing.

Runway information at Martha's Vineyard is as follows; 15 - 33 and 6 - 24

Control tower 121.4
A.T.I.S. 126.25
Ground 122.95
Field elevation 68
Unicom 122.95

We will plan our decent at about 30 N.M. from Martha's Vineyard.

We are at 5500 feet with a decent rate of 500 feet per minute, in 5 minutes we should be at 2000 feet where we will level off and look for the field.

At point of level off at 2000 feet we should be about 20 N.M. from field. We wait 10 minutes and should have the field in sight.

We will now call C.T. 121.4 and confirm active runway and landing instructions.

As the reader can see there is lots to do in making this flight.

We however, try to eliminate the unforeseen.

Good communication is the key to a successful trip.

Also if I encounter bad weather, I can just do a 180 degrees turn and go back to the last airport.

This completes our flight to (M.V.Y.), Martha's Vineyard airport.

It is a basic layout of what a pilot should do to complete this flight visit using V.F.R. As you can see, there are a lot of steps involved and, unless you've made the flight many many times, your're not likely to have all of that information at your fingertips. It would be a difficult flight to make if you were thinking that you would just hop into the plane and liftoff.

A PERSONAL ANALYSIS

Attempting a night flight to M.V.Y. on a summer evening in July, is always difficult. The weather is always subject to change, and the occurrence of smog and haze is almost a certainty. What's more, the weather pattern is erratic, it could be clear in one location and foggy or hazy in another, depending on winds.

In the 15 months before the accident JFK, Jr., (the pilot) had flown about 35 flight legs either to or from the Essex County/Teterboro, New Jersey area and Martha's Vineyard/Hyannis Massachusetts area.

The pilot flew over 17 of these legs without a C.F.I. on board, including at least 5 at night. So JFK, Jr. had to be pretty familiar with the area, its weather patterns, it's landmarks, airports, etc. The pilot also knew that the more daylight you add to the equation, the more favorable it is for the flight.

Sunset this time of year occurred about 8:14 p.m. or 2014, civil twilight ended about 2047 about 30 minutes later, and nautical twilight ended about 2128 or 9:28 p.m. Everything is pretty pitch black after nautical twilight, especially black water to black sky. So getting started early would have been a definite plus.

JFK, Jr. called the Fixed Base Operator(F.B.O.) at about 1:00 p.m., or 1300 hours, on the day of the accident to request that they park his plane outside the hanger as he was planning to arrive between 1730 and 1800 hours.

A one hour flight to (M.V.Y.) Martha's Vineyard and another 30 minutes to (H.Y.N.) Hyannis.

It would be all over by sunset. But it wasn't.

As a pilot there is always a lot of responsibility involved in any flight, many tasks have to be performed, as I have previously explained. This creates a great deal of stress, tension and anxiety. There is an added responsibility for the pilot when they have passengers aboard. With a C.F.I. on board the flight becomes less stressful. One pilot could do the flying and the other would handle the navigation and radio communication and could do an instrument approach to M.V.Y. if necessary.

His C.F.I. spoke with him earlier in the day and offered to do the flight, he declined the offer, stating "he wants to do this alone."

This thought of "doing it alone' can be one's 'undoing'. Enthusiasm to prove one's flying ability might outweigh good sense.

John also had a cast on his leg, which may have been an annoyance, as he did not have 100% free motion on the rudder controls, would have had some loss of tactile feed back.

He also knew that if (M.V.Y.), Martha's Vineyard was not visible, he might not be able to do an instrument approach by himself, as he was not instrument rated.

He also had trouble performing multiple tasks while flying. This fact was noted by his C.F.I. on one of his reports, but concentrating on flying the airplane, staying on course, and maintaining altitude was a full time job.

He had one thing which he could hope would hold, a seemingly favorable weather briefing along his route of flight. According to the Weather Service International, (W.S.I.) personnel, two weather requests from W.S.I.'s pilot brief web site were made by him or someone using his user code.

The first request made at 1832:59 was for a radar image.

The second request, made at 1834:18, was for a route briefing from T.E.B., (Teterboro) to H.Y.A., (Hyannis) with M.V.Y., (Martha's Vineyard as an alternate.

The pertinent information was that visibility along the route of flight varied from 10 miles to 4 miles in haze at C.D.W., (Caldwell). These observations were made about 1800.

Excerpts from these observations include the following:

H.Y.A. - Hyannis 1756 - few clouds at 2700 feet, visibility 6 miles in haze; winds 230 degrees at 13 knots.

M.V.Y. - Martha's Vineyard 1753 - clear skies, visibility 6 miles in haze, winds 210 degrees at 11 knots.

Also included were the following terminal forecasts for A.C.K., (Nantucket) and H.Y.A., (Hyannis).

A.C.K. (July 16 at 1400 to July 17 at 1400) July 16 1400 to 2000 clear skies; visibility greater than 6 miles; wind 240 degrees at 15 knots. Becoming 2000 to 2100, winds 260 degrees at 13 knots.

H.Y.A. (July 16 at 1400 to July 17 at 1400) July 16 1400 to 2200 clear skies; visibility greater than 6 miles; wind 230 degrees at 10 knots.

The above forecasts especially the terminal forecasts appear to be favorable, *except* the latest forecast given for M.V.Y. was at 1753, (5:53 p.m.), roughly 3 hours before his departure from C.D.W., (Caldwell). Now the problem, according to WSI, the pilot, or someone using his user code did not access the National Weather Service, (NWS) area forecast.

Aviation Forecasts and Surface Weather Observations Area Forecasts (FA)

Excerpts from the Boston FA, issued July 16 about 2045 and valid until July 17 about 0200, included the following: Coastal Waters (includes area of MVY); Scattered clouds at 2,000 feet.
Occasional visibility 3 to 5 miles in haze. Haze tops 7,000 feet.

Excerpts from the Boston FA, issued July 16 about 2045 and valid until July 17 about 0900, included the following; Coastal Waters (includes area of MVY); North of 40 degrees latitude...Scattered cirrus. Occasional visibility 4 to 5 miles in haze. Haze tops 8,000 feet.

So now at 2045, JFK Jr's approximate departure from C.D.W., visibility at M.V.Y. decreases from clear skies; visibility 6 miles in haze to scattered clouds at 2,000 feet, occasional visibility 3 to 5 miles in haze.

And what about darkness setting in to make matters worse? The time update, (TAF) forecasts as follows: Aviation Terminal Forecasts (TAF)

NWS does not prepare TAFs for MVY. Excerpts from TAF pertinent to the accident include the following:

The TAF for ACK, issued July 16 about 1330 and valid from July 16 about 1400 to July 17 about 1400, was as follows: July 16 at 1400 to July 1700 at 1100...Clear skies; visibility greater than 6 miles; winds 240 degrees at 15 knots. Becoming July 16 at 2000 to July 16 at 2100 winds 260 degrees at 13 knots.

The TAF for ACK, issued July 16 about 1930 and valid from July 16 about 2000 to July 17 about 2000, was as follows: July 16 at 2000 to July 17 at 0200...Winds 240 degrees at 15 knots; visibility 4 miles, mist; scattered clouds at 25,000 feet. Temporary changes from July 16 at 2100 to July 17 at 0100...clouds 500 feet scattered; visibility 2 miles, mist.

The TAF for HYA, issued July 16 about 1330 and valid from July 16 about 1400 to July 17 about 1400, was as follows: July 16 at 1400 to July 17 at 1100...Clear skies; visibility greater than 6 miles; winds 230 degrees at 10 knots. Winds becoming July 16 at 2200 to July 17 at 0000...250 degrees at 8 knots.

The TAF for HYA, issued July 16 about 1930 and valid from July 16 about 2000 to July 17 about 2000, was as follows: July 16 at 2000 to July 17 at 0200...Winds 230 degrees at 10 knots; visibility 6 miles; haze; scattered clouds at 9,000 feet. Temporary changes from July 16 at 2000 to July 17 at 000...Visibility 4 miles, haze.

So now we are down to a possible visibility of 2 miles in mist on an updated report.

So what JFK, Jr. thought was a favorable forecast was deteriorating fast.

Another factor to heighten the tension that evening was the traffic.

Imagine trying to depart as soon as possible, only to have route 80, backed up in traffic.

Another pilot who kept his twin turboprop airplane at TEB, and on the evening of the accident, he flew from TEB to ACK. The pilot stated that he drove to TEB from New York City and that the traffic was the second heaviest he had seen in 15 years. The pilot stated that he had called the TEB FBO and estimated that his arrival time would be about 1850; however, he did not arrive until between about 1930 and 2000 because of traffic. The pilot also stated that this delay changed the flight from one that would have been conducted entirely during the day to one that would have to be conducted partially at night. The pilot further stated, "Our car took route 80 to Teterboro airport. Caldwell airport, where (the accident pilot) flew from is another 14 minute drive west on route 80 past TEB."

Before departing the city, the pilot obtained current weather observations and forecasts for Nantucket and other points in Massachusetts, Connecticut, New York, and New Jersey. He stated that the visibility was well above VFR minimums. He also stated that he placed a telephone call to a flight service station (FSS) before leaving the city, while driving to TEB. Regarding the telephone call he stated the following: "I asked if there were any adverse conditions for the route TEB to ACK. I was told emphatically: 'No adverse conditions. Have a great weekend.' I queried the briefer about any expected fog and was told none was expected and the conditions would remain VFR with good visibility. Again, I was reassured that tonight was not a problem."

The pilot stated that he departed TEB "...in daylight and good flight conditions and reasonable visibility. The horizon was not obscured by haze. I could easily pick out land marks at least five (miles) away." The pilot also stated that he did not request or receive flight information after his departure from TEB. Once clear of the New York Class B airspace, he stated that he climbed his airplane to 17,500 feet and proceeded towards Nantucket. He reported above 14,000 feet, the visibility was unrestricted; however, he also reported that during the decent to Nantucket, when his global positioning system (GPS) receiver indicated that he was over Martha's Vineyard, he looked down and..."there was nothing to see. There was no horizon and no light...I turned left toward Martha's Vineyard to see if it was visible but could see no lights of any kind nor any evidence of the island...I thought the island might have suffered a power failure."

Getting back to the JFK, Jr. flight, it is easy to formulate the conclusion that great haste was exercised here as the correct frequencies were not dialed into some of the navigation communication radios, and after contacting Caldwell CDW Tower for departure instruction and clearance. According to Air Traffic Control, (ATC) "No records of any further communication between the pilot and ATC exist." Basic flight training; 3 C's - Communicate, Communicate, Communicate.

Both of the airplane's communication/navigation transceivers received severe impact damage and could not be powered up. The nonvolatile memory circuit chips were extracted from the transceivers, placed in a test unit, and powered up. The following information was noted about each of the transceivers:

Transceiver No. 1, KX-165

The in-use communication frequency was set at 132.02, which was the same frequency as the TEB automatic terminal information service (ATIS).

The standby communication frequency was set at 135.25; the CDW ATIS had a frequency of 135.5.

The in-use navigation frequency was set at 109.80, which was the same frequency as the New Haven, Connecticut, VOR.

Albert Pecker

The standby navigation frequency was set at 133.10, which was the same frequency as LaGuardia Airport, New York, VOR.

Transceiver No. 2, KX-165

The in-use communication frequency was set at 121.40, which is the same frequency as MVY tower.

The standby communication frequency was set at 127.25; the MVY ATIS had a frequency of 126.25.

The in-use navigation frequency was set at 108.80, which was the same frequency as the BDR VOR.

The standby navigation frequency was set at 110.00, which was the same frequency as Norwich, Connecticut, VOR.

One would draw the conclusion that the Martha's Vineyard, VOR 114.5 should have been dialed into one of the transceivers for the in-use navigation frequency, even if the GPS receiver on board was used to navigate this flight.

Before taking off all radios and navigation equipment should be set with the proper frequencies for the flight.

The radio frequencies and navigation frequencies that were dialed into the communication and navigation radios for this flight make little sense to me.

Now back to the flight.

At 2034 JFK, Jr. had all parties aboard and called the tower at CDW for takeoff direction and clearance.

Upon takeoff and leaving CDW pattern his plane headed Northeast on a course of 55 degrees toward the Hudson River.

The plane was now in New York TCA Airspace and even though the tower controller offered to notify Teterboro that JFK, Jr. was about to enter their airspace, he declined and neglected to do so himself.

It is telling that Teterboro control tower 119.5 was not dialed into one of the planes 4 communication radios, but Teterboro ATIS 132.02 was and was really not necessary for this portion of the plane trip.

Upon reaching a point about 8 miles Northwest of the Westchester County airport, (HPN) White Plains, New York, the plane turned North over the river and began to climb.

After proceeding north about 6 miles, the target, (alleged JFK, Jr.'s plane turned eastward to a course about 100 degrees. The target continued to climb and reached 5,500 feet about 6 miles northeast of HPN. When the target's course was plotted on a New York VFR navigational map, the extended course line crossed the island of Martha's Vineyard.

Still no radio communication from N9253N (JFK, Jr.'s plane), indicating pilot's intense desire to fly the airplane, to maintain visual and flight stability, example of extreme stress and concentration.

As I previously stated within 10 nautical miles of a class D airport (HPN), radio communication is required.

At the very same time as JFK, Jr.'s plane is alleged to be in the area, and not heard from, a tense drama is unfolding at HPN (Westchester County Airport).

An account of this drama is as follows:

The following TCAS alert occurred during the approach of a commercial airplane to HPN, which was located within published Class D airspace and the New York Class B airspace. On July 16, 1999, about 2049, American Airlines flight 1484, a Fokker 100, was inbound for landing at HPN. According to the transcripts of communications between flight 1484 and the New York approach controller, at 2049:33, flight 1484 was level at 6,000 feet. At 2049:48, the controller instructed flight 1484 to descend and maintain at 3000 feet, which flight 1484 acknowledged. At 2050:32, the controller issued an approach clearance to flight 1484, which flight 1484 also acknowledged. The following is an excerpt of the communications transcript between flight 1484 and the controller regarding the TACS:

2052:22, the controller, "American fourteen eighty four traffic one o'clock and five miles eastbound two thousand four hundred, unverified, appears to be climbing."

2052:29, flight 1484 "American flight fourteen eighty four we're looking."

2052:56, the controller, "fourteen eighty four traffic one o'clock and uh three miles twenty eight hundred now, unverified."

2053:02, flight 1484, "um yes we have uh (unintelligible) I think we have him here american fourteen eighty four."

2053:10, flight 1484, "I understand he's not in contact with you or anybody else."

2053:14, the controller, "uh nope doesn't not talking to anybody."

2053:27, flight 1484, "seems to be climbing through uh thirty one hundred now we just got traffic advisory here."

2053:35, the controller, "uh that's what it looks like."

2053:59, flight 1484, "uh we just had a."

Albert Pecker

2054:12, the controller, "American fourteen eighty four you can contact tower nineteen seven."

2054:15, flight 1484, "nineteen seven uh we had a resolution advisory seemed to be a single engine piper or something."

2054:21 the controller, "roger."

The event that occurred outside of New York Class B and the HPN Class D airspace, and no corrective action was reported to have been taken by the controller or flight 1484. A review of the radar data correlated the unknown target with the track of N9253N.

The target, JFK, Jr.'s plane, continued eastward at 5,500 feet, passing just north of Bridgeport, Connecticut, and crossed the shoreline between Bridgeport and New Haven, Connecticut. The target ground track continued on the 100-degree course, just south and parallel to the Connecticut and Rhode Island coastlines. After passing Point Judith, Rhode Island, the target continued over the Rhode Island Sound.

With takeoff at (8:40 p.m.), 2040 the target (JFK, Jr.'s plane) had been in the air approximately 50 minutes, and covered about 140 nautical miles and he was at 5500 feet altitude.

The flight to Point Judith thus far had been mostly over land, with favorable visibility and land lights for ground reference, which kind of gives the pilot a horizon.

Approximately 4 minutes after passing Point Judith, 54 minutes into the flight, he began his descent from 5500 feet, he was 34 nautical miles from Martha's Vineyard.

His decent rate was calculated to have varied between 400 and 800 feet per minute (FPM).

At this time the pilot had no usable outside visual reference. The land lights on his left side were no longer visible, the haze or mist over the water would obscure what little there was of nautical twilight.

The black sky and the black water blended into one black mass.

The varied, non controlled rate of descent, which if controlled could have put him in an exact position for landing at Martha's Vineyard, was not going to happen.

A feeling of desperation, helplessness and depression that sets in a situation of this magnitude must have occurred.

No lights from Martha's Vineyard could be seen.

At about (9:38), 2138, 58 minutes into the flight the target began a right turn in a southerly direction.

About 30 seconds later, the target stopped its decent at 2,200 feet and began a climb that lasted another 30 seconds. During this period of time, the target stopped the turn, and airspeed decreased to about 153KIAS. About 2139, the target leveled off at 2,500 feet and flew in a southerly direction. About 50 seconds later, the target entered a left turn and climbed to 2,600 feet. As the target continued in the left turn, it began a descent that reached a rate of about 900 fpm. When the target reached an easterly direction, it stopped turning; its rate of descent remained about 900 fpm. At 2140:15, while still in the descent, the target entered a right turn. As the target's turn rate increased, its descent rate and airspeed also increased.

The target's descent rate was eventually exceeded 4,700 fpm. The target's last radar position was recorded at 2140:34 at an altitude of 1,100 feet.

On July 20, 1999, about 2240, the airplane's wreckage was located in 120 feet of water, about 1/4 mile north of the target's last recorded radar position.

The accident occurred during the hours of darkness. In the area of and on the night of the accident, sunset occurred about 2014, Civil twilight ended about 2047, and nautical horizon at a bearing of 270.5 degrees and provided about 19 percent illumination. The location of the accident wreckage was about 41 degrees, 17 minutes, 37.2 seconds north latitude; 70 degrees, 58 minutes, 39.2 seconds west longitude.

I don't know what happened in the last 2 minutes of flight. Perhaps spatial disorientation set in, perhaps the pilot saw ground lights of some kind at Gay Head.

The information after this point is too uncertain to theorize any further.

NTSB DETAILED REPORT

NYC99MA178
HISTORY OF FLIGHT

On July 16, 1999, about 2141 eastern daylight time, a Piper PA-32R-301, Saratoga II, N9253N, was destroyed when it crashed into the Atlantic Ocean approximately 7 1/2 miles southwest of Gay Head, Martha's Vineyard, Massachusetts. The certificated private pilot and two passengers received fatal injuries. Night visual meteorological conditions (VMC) prevailed, and no flight plan had been filed for the personal flight conducted under the provisions of 14 Code of Federal Regulations (CFR) Part 91. The flight originated from Essex County Airport (CDW), Caldwell, New Jersey, and was destined for Barnstable Municipal-Boardman/Polando Field (HYA), Hyannis, Massachusetts, with a scheduled stop at Martha's Vineyard Airport (MVY), Vineyard Haven, Massachusetts.

During interviews, witnesses stated that the purpose of the flight was to fly to Martha's Vineyard to drop off one passenger and then continue to HYA. An employee of a fixed-base operator (FBO) at CDW stated that he had called the pilot about 1300 on the day of the accident to verify that the pilot intended to fly the airplane, N9253N, over the weekend. The pilot informed the employee that he did plan to fly the airplane and that he would arrive at the airport between 1730 and 1800. The employee informed the pilot that he would have the airplane parked outside of the hangar.

Witnesses who were at CDW on the night of the accident stated that they saw the pilot and a female near the accident airplane. The witnesses also reported that they saw the pilot using crutches and loading luggage into the airplane. One witness stated that he watched the pilot perform an engine run-up and then take off about 2040. The witness further stated that "takeoff and right downwind departure seem[ed] normal."

According to air traffic control (ATC) transcripts from CDW's tower, about 2034, the pilot of N9253N contacted the ground controller and stated, "...saratoga niner two five three november ready to taxi with mike...right turnout northeast bound." The ground controller instructed the pilot to taxi to runway 22, which the pilot acknowledged. At 2038:32, the pilot of N9253N contacted the tower controller and advised that he was ready to take off from runway 22. At 2038:39, the tower controller cleared N9253N for takeoff; at 2038:43, the pilot acknowledged the clearance. A few seconds later, the tower controller asked the pilot if he was heading towards Teterboro, New Jersey. The pilot replied, "No sir, I'm uh actually I'm heading a little uh north of it, uh eastbound." The tower controller then instructed the pilot to "make it a right downwind departure then." At 2038:56, the pilot acknowledged the instruction stating, "right downwind departure two two." No records of any further communications between the pilot and ATC exist.

According to radar data, at 2040:59, a target transmitting a visual flight rules (VFR) code was observed about 1 mile southwest of CDW at an altitude of 1,300 feet. The target proceeded to the northeast, on a course of about 55 degrees, remaining below 2,000 feet. The target was at 1,400 feet when it reached the Hudson River. When the target was about 8 miles northwest of the Westchester County Airport (HPN), White Plains, New York, it turned north over the river and began to climb. After proceeding north about 6 miles, the target turned eastward to a course of about 100 degrees. The target continued to climb and reached 5,500 feet about 6 miles northeast of HPN. When the target's course was plotted on a New York VFR navigational map, the extended course line crossed the island of Martha's Vineyard.

The target continued eastward at 5,500 feet, passing just north of Bridgeport, Connecticut, and crossed the shoreline between Bridgeport and New Haven, Connecticut. The target ground track continued on the 100-degree course, just south and parallel to the Connecticut and Rhode Island coastlines. After passing Point Judith, Rhode Island, the target continued over the Rhode Island Sound.

A performance study of the radar data revealed that the target began a descent from 5,500 feet about 34 miles west of MVY. The speed during the descent was calculated to be about 160 knots indicated airspeed (KIAS), and the rate of descent was calculated to have varied between 400 and 800 feet per minute (fpm). About 2138, the target began a right turn in a southerly direction. About 30 seconds later, the target stopped its descent at 2,200 feet and began a climb that lasted another 30 seconds. During this period of time, the target stopped the turn, and the airspeed decreased to about 153 KIAS. About 2139, the target leveled off at 2,500 feet and flew in a southeasterly direction. About 50 seconds later, the target entered a left turn and climbed to 2,600 feet. As the target continued in the left turn, it began a descent that reached a rate of about 900 fpm. When the target reached an easterly direction, it stopped turning; its rate of descent remained about 900 fpm. At 2140:15, while still in the descent, the target entered a right turn. As the target's turn rate increased, its descent rate and airspeed also increased. The target's descent rate eventually exceeded 4,700 fpm. The target's last radar position was recorded at 2140:34 at an altitude of 1,100 feet. (For a more detailed description of the target's [accident airplane's] performance, see Section, "Tests and Research," Subsection, "Aircraft Performance Study.")

On July 20, 1999, about 2240, the airplane's wreckage was located in 120 feet of water, about 1/4 mile north of the target's last recorded radar position.

The accident occurred during the hours of darkness. In the area of and on the night of the accident, sunset occurred about 2014. Civil twilight ended about 2047, and nautical twilight ended about 2128. About 2140, the moon was about 11.5 degrees above the horizon at a bearing of 270.5 degrees and provided about 19 percent illumination. The location of the accident wreckage was about 41 degrees, 17 minutes, 37.2 seconds north latitude; 70 degrees, 58 minutes, 39.2 seconds west longitude.

PILOT INFORMATION

The pilot obtained his private pilot certificate for "airplane single-engine land" in April 1998. He did not possess an instrument rating. He received a "high performance airplane" sign-off in his Cessna 182 in June 1998 and a "complex airplane" sign-off in the accident airplane in May 1999. His most recent Federal Aviation Administration (FAA) second-class medical certificate was issued on December 27, 1997, with no limitations.

A copy of the pilot's logbook that covered from October 4, 1982, to November 11, 1998, was provided to the Safety Board. The pilot's most recent logbook was not located. The Board used the copied logbook, records from training facilities, copies of flight instructors' logbooks, and statements from instructors and pilots to estimate the pilot's total flight experience. The pilot's estimated total flight experience, excluding simulator training, was about 310 hours, of which 55 hours were at night. The pilot's estimated experience flying without a certified flight instructor (CFI) on board was about 72 hours. The pilot's estimated flight time in the accident airplane was about 36 hours, of which 9.4 hours were at night. Approximately 3 hours of that flight time was without a CFI on board, and about 0.8 hour of that time was flown at night, which included a night landing. In the 15 months before the accident, the pilot had flown about 35 flight legs either to or from the Essex County/Teterboro, New Jersey, area and the Martha's Vineyard/Hyannis, Massachusetts, area. The pilot flew over 17 of these legs without a CFI on board, including at least 5 at night. The pilot's last known flight in the accident airplane without a CFI on board was on May 28, 1999.

Pilot Training

On October 4, 1982, the pilot started receiving flight instruction. Over the next 6 years, he flew with six different CFIs. During this period, the pilot logged 47 hours, consisting of 46 hours of dual instruction and 1 hour without a CFI on board. The pilot made no entries in his logbook from September 1988 to December 1997.

In December 1997, the pilot enrolled in a training program at Flight Safety International (FSI), Vero Beach, Florida, to obtain his private pilot certificate. Between December 1997 and April 1998, the pilot flew about 53 hours, of which 43 were flown with a

CFI on board. The CFI who prepared the pilot for his private pilot checkride stated that the pilot had "very good" flying skills for his level of experience.

On April 22, 1998, the pilot passed his private pilot flight test. The designated pilot examiner who administered the checkride stated that as part of the flight test, the pilot conducted two unusual attitude recoveries. The pilot examiner stated that in both cases, the pilot recovered the airplane while wearing a hood and referencing the airplane's flight instruments. After receiving his private pilot certificate, the pilot flew solo in his Cessna 182 and received instruction in it by CFIs local to New Jersey. He also received instruction at Million Air, a flight school in New Jersey, and flew their airplanes. During calendar year 1998, the pilot flew approximately 179 hours, including about 65 hours without a CFI on board. On March 12, 1999, the pilot completed the FAA's written airplane instrument examination and received a score of 78 percent.

On April 5, 1999, the pilot returned to FSI to begin an airplane instrument rating course. During the instrument training, the pilot satisfactorily completed the first 12 of 25 lesson plans. The pilot's primary CFI during the instrument training stated that the pilot's progression was normal and that he grasped all of the basic skills needed to complete the course; however, the CFI did recall the pilot having difficulty completing lesson 11, which was designed to develop a student's knowledge of very high frequency omnidirectional radio range (VOR) and nondirectional beacon operations while working with ATC. It took the pilot four attempts to complete lesson 11 satisfactorily. After two of the attempts, the pilot took a 1-week break. After this break, the pilot repeated lesson 11 two more times. The CFI stated that the pilot's basic instrument flying skills and simulator work were excellent. However, the CFI stated that the pilot had trouble managing multiple tasks while flying, which he felt was normal for the pilot's level of experience.

The pilot attended this training primarily on weekends. During this training, the pilot accumulated 13.3 hours of flight time with a CFI on board. In addition, the pilot logged 16.9 hours of simulator time. The pilot departed from FSI for the last time on April 24, 1999.

The pilot continued to receive flight instruction from CFIs in New Jersey in his newly purchased Piper Saratoga, the accident airplane. One CFI flew with the pilot on three occasions. One of the flights was on June 25, 1999, from CDW to MVY. The CFI stated that the departure, en route, and descent portions of the flight were executed in VMC, but an instrument approach was required into MVY because of a 300-foot overcast ceiling. The CFI requested an instrument flight rules (IFR) clearance and demonstrated a coupled instrument landing system (ILS) approach to runway 24. The CFI stated that the pilot performed the landing, but he had to assist with the rudders because of the pilot's injured ankle. (For additional information about the pilot's ankle injury, see Section, "Medical and Pathological Information.") The CFI stated that the pilot's aeronautical abilities and his ability to handle multiple tasks while flying were average for his level of experience.

A second CFI flew with the pilot between May 1998 and July 1999. This CFI accumulated 39 hours of flight time with the pilot, including 21 hours of night flight and 0.9 hour flown in instrument meteorological conditions (IMC). The pilot used this CFI for instruction on cross-country flights and as a safety pilot. On July 1, 1999, the CFI flew with the pilot in the accident airplane to MVY. The flight was conducted at night, and IMC prevailed at the airport. The CFI stated that, during the flight, the pilot used and seemed competent with the autopilot. The instructor added that during the flight the pilot was wearing a nonplaster cast on his leg, which required the CFI to taxi the airplane and assist the pilot with the landing.

The CFI stated that the pilot had the ability to fly the airplane without a visible horizon but may have had difficulty performing additional tasks under such conditions. He also stated that the pilot was not ready for an instrument evaluation as of July 1, 1999, and needed additional training. The CFI was not aware of the pilot conducting any flight in the accident airplane without an instructor on board. He also stated that he would not have felt comfortable with the accident pilot conducting night flight operations on a route similar to the one flown on, and in weather conditions similar to those that existed on, the night of the accident. The CFI further stated that he had talked to the pilot on the day of the accident and offered to fly with him on the accident flight. He stated that the accident pilot replied that "he wanted to do it alone."

A third CFI flew with the pilot between May 1998 and July 1999. This CFI accumulated 57 hours of flight time with the pilot, including 17 hours of night flight and 8 hours flown in IMC. The pilot also used this instructor for instruction on cross-country flights and as a safety pilot. This CFI had conducted a "complex airplane" evaluation on the pilot and signed him off in the accident airplane in May 1999. According to the CFI, on one or two occasions, the airplane's autopilot turned to a heading other than the one selected, which required the autopilot to be disengaged and then reengaged. He stated that it seemed as if the autopilot had independently changed from one navigation mode to another. He also stated that he did not feel that the problem was significant because it only happened once or twice.

The CFI had made six or seven flights to MVY with the pilot in the accident airplane. The CFI stated that most of the flights were conducted at night and that, during the flights, the pilot did not have any trouble flying the airplane. The instructor stated that the pilot was methodical about his flight planning and that he was very cautious about his aviation decision-making. The CFI stated that the pilot had the capability to conduct a night flight to MVY as long as a visible horizon existed.

AIRCRAFT INFORMATION

The accident airplane, N9253N, was a Piper PA-32R-301, Saratoga II, single-engine, low-wing airplane with retractable landing gear. The airplane was originally certificated by Piper Aircraft Corporation on June 9, 1995. The airplane was sold to Skytech, Inc., Baltimore, Maryland, on June 16, 1995, and then resold to Poinciana LLC, Wilmington, North Carolina, on January 5, 1996.

A review of records from an engine overhaul facility revealed that during a 100-hour and annual inspection of the airplane in May 1998, corrosion was observed on the interior surfaces of the engine cylinder walls. Additionally, pitting was observed on the surfaces of several valve tappets. At that time, the engine had a total time since new of 387.1 hours. The documents also revealed that the engine was shipped to the overhaul facility in June 1998, where the engine was disassembled, inspected, and reassembled (parts were replaced as necessary) in June and July 1998. The engine was also run in a test cell before it was shipped and was reinstalled in the airplane in July 1998.

On August 25, 1998, the airplane was purchased by Raytheon Aircraft Company, Wichita, Kansas, and then resold the same day to Air Bound Aviation, Inc., Fairfield, New Jersey. The airplane was sold on

August 27, 1998, to a pilot in New Jersey. On April 28, 1999, the airplane was sold to Columbia Aircraft Sales, Inc., Groton, Connecticut. On the same day, the airplane was sold back to Air Bound Aviation and then to the accident pilot, operating as Random Ventures, Inc., New York, New York. According to maintenance personnel at CDW, the pilot kept the airplane's maintenance records inside of the airplane. The maintenance records were not recovered during the wreckage recovery operation.

According to FAA records, work orders, and a statement from an employee of a maintenance facility, a prepurchase inspection of N9253N was conducted on April 16, 1999. According to the maintenance facility employee, "the aircraft was found to be in very good condition, with only a few minor discrepancies." According to the records and the maintenance facility employee, an annual inspection was completed on June 18, 1999, at a total airframe time of 622.8 hours, and the airplane was returned to service on June 25, 1999. The records and maintenance facility employee also revealed that the airplane's return to service was delayed because of an error on the airplane's registration form about its exact make and model. A new registration form with the correct information had to be sent to the pilot for his signature.

A July 13, 1999, work order revealed that a "swing" of the compass and the horizontal situation indicator (HSI) were completed. No total airframe time was recorded on that work order. The tachometer recovered in the wreckage indicated 663.5 hours.

A review of other pilots' logbooks revealed that they had flown the airplane without the accident pilot on board. However, it could not be accurately determined how many other pilots might have flown the airplane without the pilot on board or how many flight hours they might have added on to the airplane.

METEOROLOGICAL INFORMATION

The following airport designators (and those previously defined) are used in this section:

ACK - Nantucket Memorial Airport, Nantucket, Massachusetts.

BDR - Igor I. Sikorsky Memorial Airport, Bridgeport, Connecticut.

BID - Block Island State Airport, Block Island, Rhode Island.

BLM - Allaire Airport, Belmar-Farmingdale, New Jersey.

EWB - New Bedford Municipal Airport, New Bedford, Massachusetts.

EWR - Newark International Airport, Newark, New Jersey.

FMH - Otis ANGB, Falmouth, Massachusetts.

FOK - Francis S. Gabreski Airport, Westhampton Beach, New York.

FRG - Republic Airport, Farmingdale, New York.

ISP - Long Island MacArthur Airport, Islip, New York.

JFK - John F. Kennedy International Airport, New York, New York.

PVD - Theodore Francis Green State Airport, Providence, Rhode Island.

TAN - Taunton Municipal, Taunton, Massachusetts.

TEB - Teterboro Airport, Teterboro, New Jersey.

ACK is located about 27 nautical miles (nm) east-southeast of MVY. HYA is located about 22 nm northeast of MVY.

Pilot Preflight Weather Requests

According to Weather Service International (WSI) personnel, a search of their briefing logs indicated that the pilot, or someone using his user code, made two weather requests from WSI's PILOTbrief Web site on July 16, 1999. The first request, made at 1832:59, was for a radar image. The second request, made at 1834:18, was for a route briefing from TEB to HYA with MVY as an alternate.

The information provided to the requester included en route weather observations from BID, BLM, EWB, EWR, FMH, FOK, FRG, ISP, JFK, PVD, and TAN. These observations indicated that visibilities varied from 10 miles along the route to 4 miles in haze at CDW. The lowest cloud ceiling was reported at 20,000 feet overcast at PVD. These observations were made about 1800. Observations for ACK, CDW, HYA, and MVY were also included. Excerpts from these observations include the following:

ACK 1753...Clear skies; visibility 5 miles in mist; winds 240 degrees at 16 knots.

CDW 1753...Clear skies; visibility 4 miles in haze; winds 230 degrees at 7 knots.

HYA 1756...Few clouds at 7,000 feet; visibility 6 miles in haze; winds 230 degrees at 13 knots.

MVY 1753...Clear skies; visibility 6 miles in haze; winds 210 degrees at 11 knots.

Also included were the following terminal forecasts for ACK and HYA:

ACK (July 16 at 1400 to July 17 at 1400)...July 16...1400 to 2000...Clear skies; visibility greater than 6 miles; winds 240 degrees at 15 knots. Becoming 2000 to 2100, winds 260 degrees at 13 knots.

HYA (July 16 at 1400 to July 17 at 1400)...July 16...1400 to 2200...Clear skies; visibility greater than 6 miles; winds 230 degrees at 10 knots.

According to WSI, the pilot, or someone using his user code, did not access the National Weather Service (NWS) Area Forecast.

Aviation Forecasts and Surface Weather Observations Area Forecasts (FA)

Excerpts from the Boston FA, issued July 16 about 2045 and valid until July 17 about 0200, included the following: Coastal Waters (includes area of MVY);

Scattered clouds at 2,000 feet. Occasional visibility 3 to 5 miles in haze. Haze tops 7,000 feet.

Excerpts from the Boston FA, issued July 16 about 2045 and valid until July 17 about 0900, included the following: Coastal Waters (includes area of MVY); North of 40 degrees north latitude...Scattered cirrus. Occasional visibility 4 to 5 miles in haze. Haze tops 8,000 feet.

Aviation Terminal Forecasts (TAF)

NWS does not prepare TAFs for MVY. Excerpts from TAFs pertinent to the accident include the following:

The TAF for ACK, issued July 16 about 1330 and valid from July 16 about 1400 to July 17 about 1400, was as follows: July 16 at 1400 to July 17 at 1100...Clear skies; visibility greater than 6 miles; winds 240 degrees at 15 knots. Becoming July 16 at 2000 to July 16 at 2100, winds 260 degrees at 13 knots.

The TAF for ACK, issued July 16 about 1930 and valid from July 16 about 2000 to July 17 about 2000, was as follows: July 16 at 2000 to July 17 at 0200...Winds 240 degrees at 15 knots; visibility 4 miles, mist; scattered clouds at 25,000 feet. Temporary changes from July 16 at 2100 to July 17 at 0100...clouds 500 feet scattered; visibility 2 miles, mist.

The TAF for HYA, issued July 16 about 1330 and valid from July 16 about 1400 to July 17 about 1400, was as follows: July 16 at 1400 to July 17 at 1100...Clear skies; visibility greater than 6 miles; winds 230 degrees at 10 knots. Winds becoming July 16 at 2200 to July 17 at 0000...250 degrees at 8 knots.

The TAF for HYA, issued July 16 about 1930 and valid from July 16 about 2000 to July 17 about 2000, was as follows: July 16 at 2000 to July 17 at 0200...Winds 230 degrees at 10 knots; visibility 6 miles, haze; scattered clouds at 9,000 feet. Temporary changes from July 16 at 2000 to July 17 at 0000...Visibility 4 miles, haze.

In-flight Weather Advisories

No airmen's meteorological information, significant meteorological information (SIGMET), or convective SIGMETs were issued by the NWS Aviation Weather Center in Kansas City, Missouri, for the time and area of the accident. No in-flight weather advisories were in effect along the route between CDW and MVY from 2000 to 2200.

Surface Weather Observations

MVY had an Automated Surface Observing System (ASOS), which was edited and augmented by ATC tower personnel if necessary. The tower manager at MVY was on duty on the night of the accident for an

8-hour shift, which ended when the tower closed, about 2200. During an interview, the tower manager stated that no actions were taken to augment or edit the ASOS during his shift. He also stated the following:

"The visibility, present weather, and sky condition at the approximate time of the accident was probably a little better than what was being reported. I say this because I remember aircraft on visual approaches saying they had the airport in sight between 10 and 12 miles out. I do recall being able to see those aircraft and I do remember seeing the stars out that night...To the best of my knowledge, the ASOS was working as advertised that day with no reported problems or systems log errors."

ASOS observations for the night of the accident include the following:

ACK

2053...Clear at or below 12,000 feet; visibility 4 miles, mist; winds 240 degrees at 11 knots; temperature 21 degrees [Celsius] C; dewpoint 20 degrees C; altimeter setting 30.10 inches of [mercury] Hg.

2153...Clear at or below 12,000 feet; visibility 4 miles, mist; winds 240 degrees at 12 knots; temperature 21 degrees C; dewpoint 20 degrees C; altimeter setting 30.11 inches of Hg.

Albert Pecker

BDR

2054...Clear at or below 12,000 feet; visibility 8 miles, haze; winds 230 degrees at 4 knots; temperature 27 degrees C; dewpoint 21 degrees C; altimeter setting 30.08 inches of Hg.

CDW

1953...Clear at or below 12,000 feet; visibility 4 miles, haze; winds 230 degrees at 4 knots; temperature 33 degrees C; dewpoint 18 degrees C; altimeter setting 30.07 inches of Hg.

2053...Clear at or below 12,000 feet; visibility 5 miles, haze; winds 220 degrees at 5 knots; temperature 31 degrees C; dewpoint 19 degrees C; altimeter setting 30.08 inches of Hg.

HPN

2045...7,500 feet broken, 15,000 feet overcast, visibility 5 miles haze; winds 140 degrees at 4 knots; temperature 28 degrees C; dewpoint 22 degrees C; altimeter setting 30.08 inches of Hg.

HYA

2056...Few clouds at 7,000 feet; visibility 6 miles, mist; winds 230 degrees at 7 knots;temperature 23 degrees C; dewpoint 21 degrees C; altimeter setting 30.07 inches of Hg.

2156...Few clouds at 7,500 feet; visibility 6 miles, mist; winds 230 degrees at 8 knots; temperature 23 degrees C; dewpoint 22 degrees C; altimeter setting 30.08 inches of Hg.

MVY

2053...Clear at or below 12,000 feet; visibility 8 miles; winds 250 degrees at 7 knots; temperature 23 degrees C; dewpoint 19 degrees C; altimeter 30.09 inches of Hg.

2153...Clear at or below 12,000 feet; visibility 10 miles; winds 240 degrees at 10 knots, gusts to 15 knots; temperature 24 degrees C; dewpoint 18 degrees C; altimeter 30.10 inches of Hg.

U.S. Coast Guard Station (USCG) Weather Observations

Safety Board staff reviewed weather observations from USCG stations. Excerpts pertinent to the accident include the following:

Point Judith, Rhode Island
1700...Cloudy, 3 miles visibility in haze, winds south-southwest at 10 knots.

2000...Cloudy, 3 miles visibility in haze, winds south-southwest at 10 knots.

2300...Cloudy, 2 miles visibility, winds southwest at 10 knots.

Brant Point, Massachusetts
1700...Clear, 8 miles visibility.
2000...Overcast, 6 miles visibility.
2300...Scattered clouds, 6 miles visibility.

The Brant Point report stated that two observations were reported by ships. About 2000, a ship 1 nm north of buoy 17, which was about 8 miles north of Martha's Vineyard, reported that the seas were 2 to 3 feet and that the visibility was 5 nm. About 2300, another ship reported that the winds were west-southwest at 10 to 15 knots, the seas were 2 to 3 feet, and the visibility was 6 nm in light haze.

Pilot Weather Observations

Three pilots who had flown over the Long Island Sound on the night of the accident were interviewed after the accident.

One pilot kept his twin turboprop airplane at TEB, and on the evening of the accident, he flew from TEB to ACK. The pilot stated that he drove to TEB from New York City and that the traffic was the second heaviest he had seen in 15 years. The pilot stated that he had called the TEB FBO and estimated that his arrival time would be about 1850; however, he did not arrive until between about 1930 and 2000 because of traffic. The pilot also stated that this delay changed the flight from one that would have been conducted entirely during the day to one that would have to be conducted partially at night. The pilot further stated, "Our car took route 80 to Teterboro Airport. Caldwell Airport, where [the accident pilot] flew from is another 14 minute drive west on route 80 past TEB."

Before departing the city, the pilot had obtained current weather observations and forecasts for Nantucket and other points in Massachusetts, Connecticut, New York, and New Jersey. He stated that the visibility was well above VFR minimums. He also stated that he placed a telephone call to a flight service station (FSS) before leaving the city, while driving to TEB. Regarding the telephone call, he stated the following:

"I asked if there were any adverse conditions for the route TEB to ACK. I was told emphatically: 'No adverse conditions. Have a great weekend.' I queried the briefer about any expected fog and was told none was expected and the conditions would remain VFR with good visibility. Again, I was reassured that tonight was not a problem."

The pilot stated that he departed TEB "...in daylight and good flight conditions and reasonable visibility. The horizon was not obscured by haze. I could easily pick our land marks at least five [miles] away." The pilot also stated that he did not request or receive flight information after his departure from TEB. Once clear of the New York Class B airspace, he stated that he climbed his airplane to 17,500 feet and proceeded towards Nantucket. He reported that above

113

14,000 feet, the visibility was unrestricted; however, he also reported that during his descent to Nantucket, when his global positioning system (GPS) receiver indicated that he was over Martha's Vineyard, he looked down and "...there was nothing to see. There was no horizon and no light...I turned left toward Martha's Vineyard to see if it was visible but could see no lights of any kind nor any evidence of the island...I thought the island might [have] suffered a power failure."

He stated that he had his strobe lights on during the descent and that at no time did they illuminate clouds or fog. He also stated, "I had no visual reference of any kind yet was free of any clouds or fog." The pilot stated that when he contacted the ACK tower for landing, he was instructed to fly south of Nantucket about 5 miles to join the downwind for runway 24; however, he maintained a distance of 3 to 4 miles because he could not see the island at 5 miles. The pilot stated that, as he neared the airport, he had to make a 310-degree turn for spacing. He stated that, during the turn, "I found that I could not hold altitude by outside reference and had to use my [vertical speed indicator] VSI and HSI to hold altitude and properly coordinate the turn."

Another pilot had flown from Bar Harbor, Maine, to Long Island, New York, and crossed the Long Island Sound on the same evening, about 1930. This pilot stated that during his preflight weather briefing from an FSS, the specialist indicated VMC for his flight. The pilot filed an IFR flight plan and conducted the flight at 6,000 feet. He stated that he encountered visibilities of 2 to 3 miles throughout the flight because of haze. He also stated that the lowest visibility was over water, between Cape Cod, Massachusetts, and eastern Long Island. He stated that he did not encounter any clouds below 6,000 feet.

A third pilot departed TEB about 2030 destined for Groton, Connecticut, after a stopover at MVY. He stated that, after departure, he flew south of HPN and, remaining clear of the Class B airspace, he climbed to 7,500 feet. He also stated that, while en route, he monitored several ATC frequencies, but did not transmit on any of them until he neared MVY. His route of flight took him over the north shore of Long Island to Montauk, New York. He stated that he then crossed over Block Island, Rhode Island, and proceeded directly to MVY.

He stated that the entire flight was conducted under VFR, with a visibility of 3 to 5 miles in haze. He stated that, over land, he could see lights on the ground when he looked directly down or slightly forward; however, he stated that, over water, there was no horizon to reference. He stated that he was not sure if he was on top of the haze layer at 7,500 feet and that, during the flight, he did not encounter any cloud layers or ground fog during climb or descent. He further stated that, between Block Island and MVY, there was still no horizon to reference. He recalled that he began to observe lights on Martha's Vineyard when he was in the vicinity of Gay Head. He stated that, before reaching MVY, he would have begun his descent from 7,500 feet and would have been between 3,000 and 5,000 feet over Gay Head (the pilot could not recall his exact altitudes). He did not recall seeing the Gay Head marine lighthouse. He was about 4 miles from MVY when he first observed the airport's rotating beacon. He stated that he had an uneventful landing at MVY about 2145.

About 2200, the pilot departed MVY as the controller announced that the tower was closing. After takeoff, he proceeded on a heading of 290 degrees, climbed to 6,500 feet, and proceeded directly to Groton. The pilot stated that, during the return flight, the visibility was the same as that which he had encountered during the flight to MVY, which was about 3 to 5 miles in haze.

Another pilot at CDW had stated to the news media that he cancelled his planned flight from CDW to MVY on the evening of the accident because of the "poor" weather. In a written statement he stated the following:

"From my own judgement visibility appeared to be approximately 4 miles-extremely hazy. Winds were fairly light. Based only on the current weather conditions at CDW, the fact that I could not get my friends to come with me, and the fact that I would not have to spend money on a hotel room in Martha's

Vineyard, I made the decision to fly my airplane to Martha's Vineyard on Saturday."

COMMUNICATIONS

No record exists of the pilot, or a pilot using the airplane's registration number, receiving a weather briefing or filing a flight plan with any FAA FSS for the accident flight. Further, no record exists of the pilot, or a pilot using the airplane's registration number, contacting any FSS or ATC tower or facility during the duration of the flight, except for those at CDW.

The MVY ATC tower tape revealed that, during the period of time from when the accident airplane departed CDW until the tower closed and the recorder was turned off (about 2200), no contact was attempted by the pilot, the call sign of N9253N, or any unknown station.

TRAFFIC ALERT AND COLLISION AVOIDANCE SYSTEM (TCAS) ALERT NEAR HPN

According to the Aeronautical Informational Manual (AIM), definitions for Class B and D airspace are as follows:

Class B Airspace: "Generally, that airspace from the surface to 10,000 feet MSL [mean sea level], surrounding the nation's busiest airports in terms of

IFR operations or passenger enplanements...An ATC clearance is required for all aircraft to operate in the area, and all aircraft that are so cleared receive separation services within the airspace...Regardless of weather conditions, an ATC clearance is required prior to operating within Class B airspace..."

Class D Airspace: "Generally, that airspace from the surface to 2,500 feet above the airport elevation (charted in MSL) surrounding those airports that have an operational control tower...Two-way radio communication must be established with the ATC facility providing ATC services prior to entry and thereafter maintain those communications while in the Class D airspace..."

The following TCAS alert occurred during the approach of a commercial airplane to HPN, which was located within published Class D airspace and the New York Class B airspace. On July 16, 1999, about 2049, American Airlines flight 1484, a Fokker 100, was inbound for landing at HPN. According to the transcripts of communications between flight 1484 and the New York approach controller, at 2049:33, flight 1484 was level at 6,000 feet. At 2049:48, the controller instructed flight 1484 to descend and maintain 3,000 feet, which flight 1484 acknowledged. At 2050:32, the controller issued an approach clearance to flight 1484, which flight 1484 also acknowledged. The following is an excerpt of the communications transcript between flight 1484 and the controller regarding the TCAS:

2052:22, the controller, "American fourteen eighty four traffic one o'clock and five miles eastbound two thousand four hundred, unverified, appears to be climbing."

2052:29, flight 1484, "American fourteen eighty four we're looking."

2052:56, the controller, "fourteen eighty four traffic one o'clock and uh three miles twenty eight hundred now, unverified."

2053:02, flight 1484, "um yes we have uh (unintelligible) I think we have him here american fourteen eighty four."

2053:10, flight 1484, "I understand he's not in contact with you or anybody else."

2053:14, the controller, "uh nope doesn't not talking to anybody."

2053:27, flight 1484, "seems to be climbing through uh thirty one hundred now we just got a traffic advisory here."

2053:35, the controller, "uh that's what it looks like."

2053:59, flight 1484, "uh we just had a."

2054:12, the controller, "American fourteen eighty four you can contact tower nineteen seven."

2054:15, flight 1484, "nineteen seven uh we had a resolution advisory seemed to be a single engine piper er commanche or something."

2054:21, the controller, "roger."

The event occurred outside of the New York Class B and the HPN Class D airspace, and no corrective action was reported to have been taken by the controller or flight 1484. A review of the radar data correlated the unknown target with the track of N9253N.

AIRPORT INFORMATION

MVY had a field elevation of 68 feet. The hours of operation for the contract-operated tower were from 0600 to 2200. MVY had two runways. Runway 06/24 was asphalt-surfaced, 5,500 feet long, and 100 feet wide. Runway 15/33 was asphalt-surfaced, 3,297 feet long, and 75 feet wide. A VOR-distance measuring equipment (DME) navigation aid was located on the airport. The VOR was listed with a normal anticipated interference-free service of 40 nm, up to 18,000 feet with DME. ILS, VOR, and GPS instrument approaches were published for the airport.

MVY was located about 10 miles east of Gay Head. Gay Head had a lighthouse for marine navigation at 41 degrees, 20.9 minutes north latitude; 70 degrees, 50.1 minutes west longitude. According to USCG personnel, the top of the lighthouse was 170 feet above mean low water and operated 24 hours-a-day. The rotating beacon ran on a 15-second cycle, 7.3 seconds white and 7.3 seconds red. The expected range of the white light was 24 miles, and the expected range of the red light was 20 miles.

FLIGHT RECORDERS

The airplane was equipped with a Flightcom Digital Voice Recorder Clock, DVR 300i. The unit contained a digital clock, was wired into the radio communications circuits, and could record conversations between the airplane and other radio sources, ground, or air. The unit was voice activated, and the continuous loop could record and retain a total of 5 minutes of data. The unit had a nonvolatile speech memory that required a 9-volt backup battery to preserve the speech data. When the unit was located in the wreckage, it was crushed, its backup battery was missing, and it had retained no data.

WRECKAGE INFORMATION

On July 20, 1999, the airplane wreckage was located by U.S. Navy divers from the recovery ship, USS Grasp, at a depth of about 120 feet below the surface of the Atlantic Ocean. According to the divers, the recovered wreckage had been distributed in a debris field about 120 feet long and was oriented along a magnetic bearing of about 010/190 degrees. The main cabin area was found in the middle of the debris field.

A Safety Board investigator was present on the USS Grasp during the salvage operation. On July 21, 1999, the main cabin area was raised and placed aboard the USS Grasp. On July 22, 1999, the divers made five additional dives, and the wreckage retrieved from these dives was also placed aboard the USS Grasp. On July 23, 1999, about 2100, the wreckage was transferred from the USS Grasp to the Safety Board at a naval base in Newport, Rhode Island. The wreckage was then transported to the USCG Air Station at Otis Air Force Base, Cape Cod, Massachusetts, the evening of July 23, 1999. The wreckage was examined by Board investigators in a hangar at the USCG Air Station on July 24, 25, and 26, 1999. Follow-up examinations were conducted on August 1 and 2, 1999.

According to the Airworthiness Group Chairman's Report, the engine was found separated from the engine mount truss. The structural tubing on the right side of the engine mount truss was missing. The engine mount truss was deformed to the right and fractured in numerous locations. The upper left engine mount ear and both lower mount ears were fractured. The upper right engine mount ear was bent. The engine and propeller were retained for additional examination.

About 75 percent of the fuselage structure was recovered. A section of the aft cabin roof, about 5 feet long by 3 1/2 feet wide, had separated from the fuselage; this section included the airframe-mounted hinge of the left-side cargo door and a partial frame of the left-side cabin door. The left side of this section exhibited accordion crush damage in the aft direction and contained multiple folds about 5 inches deep. No fuselage structure from the left or right side of the cabin area was recovered, except for a piece of skin, about 2 feet by 2 feet, located beneath the left-side passenger window frame. The belly skin and floor structure of the fuselage were intact aft of the wing spar box carry-through section. The recovered floor structure forward of this section was fragmented. Portions of five of the six seats were found inside the fuselage. The sixth seat was not recovered. Most of the fuselage structure aft of the cabin area was recovered.

About 60 percent of the right wing structure was recovered, including the entire span of the main spar. The right wing had separated into multiple pieces and exhibited more damage than the left wing. The right wing main spar had separated into three pieces. The wing spar had fractured at its attachment to the main carry-through section. The upper spar cap fracture exhibited tension on its forward edge and compression on its aft edge. The spar web exhibited aft bending and tearing in this area.

The outboard portion of the wing leading edge exhibited rearward accordion crush damage and was separated from the remainder of the wing. No evidence of upward spar bending damage was found. No evidence of metal fatigue was found in any of the fracture surfaces.

The entire span of the right flap was recovered; it had separated into two sections (chordwise fracture), and both sections had separated from the right wing. Neither flap section exhibited bowing, bulging, or planar deformation. About 33 inches of the right aileron was recovered, and the leading edge of this section exhibited rearward crush deformation.

About 80 percent of the left wing structure was recovered, including the entire span of the main spar. The left wing main spar had separated into several pieces and exhibited less deformation than the right wing. The wing spar was fractured near the left edge of the main carry-through section. The upper and lower spar cap fractures in this area exhibited tension on the forward edges and compression on the aft edges. The spar web also exhibited aft bending and tearing in this area. No evidence of upward spar bending damage was found. No evidence of metal fatigue was found in any of the fracture surfaces.

About 90 percent of the upper and lower wing skin between the main and rear spars was recovered. The upper skin near the left wing tip was flattened out. The leading edge skin near the inboard portion of the left wing, near the stall warning port, exhibited damage consistent with uniform hydrodynamic deformation in the aft direction.

A 27-inch inboard section of the wing flap section was recovered, and the leading edge of this section exhibited aft accordion crush damage. The flap section did not exhibit any bowing, bulging, or planar deformation. The entire span of the left aileron was recovered; it had separated into two pieces. The outboard section of the aileron was curled downward.

The vertical stabilizer and rudder had separated from the aft fuselage. The stabilator had separated from the aft fuselage attach points and had fractured into five pieces. Two of the pieces consisted of left and right outboard sections, about 22 inches long, and exhibited symmetrical aft crush marks that were semicircular, with diameters of about 5 inches. The fracture surfaces of the left outboard section exhibited tearing in the aft direction. The fracture surfaces of the right outboard sections exhibited forward and upward tearing. The left inboard section of the stabilator was more intact than the right inboard section. The leading edge of the right stabilator section exhibited rearward uniform crush damage along its entire leading edge.

The lower portion of the rudder had separated from the vertical stabilizer fin structure and remained attached to the torque tube bellcrank assembly and fin aft spar. The rudder was folded over toward the right side of the airplane. The vertical stabilizer was also twisted, bent, and curled around toward the right. The structure surrounding the dorsal fin area was deformed symmetrically upward.

All three landing gear assemblies had separated from the airframe and were recovered. The retraction/extension actuating cylinders associated with the nose gear and the left main gear were found in the fully retracted position. The retraction/extension actuating cylinder for the right main gear was not recovered.

Examination of the aileron control cable circuit and associated hardware did not reveal any evidence of a preexisting jam or failure. Flight control cable continuity for the entire right aileron control circuit, including the entire balance cable that links the right aileron to the left aileron, was established. The control cable continuity for the left aileron could not be established because of impact damage and fragmentation. All of the ends of the separations of the aileron control cable circuits exhibited evidence of tensile overload. The stops for the ailerons were examined; no evidence of severe repetitive strike marks or deformations was noted.

Examination of the stabilator control cable circuit and associated hardware did not reveal any evidence of a preexisting jam or failure. Flight control cable continuity for the stabilator was established from the control surfaces to the cockpit controls. The stabilator balance weight had separated from the stabilator, and the fractures associated with the separation were consistent with tensile overload. The stops for the stabilator were examined; no evidence of severe repetitive strike marks or deformations was noted.

Examination of the stabilator trim control cable circuit and associated hardware did not reveal any evidence of a preexisting jam or failure. Control cable circuitry for the stabilator trim was established from the control surfaces to the cockpit area. An examination of the stabilator trim barrel jackscrew revealed that one full thread was protruding out of the upper portion of the trim barrel assembly housing. The barrel assembly was free to rotate and had the trim control cable wrapped around it. The two cable ends were separated about 41 inches and 37 inches, respectively, from the barrel assembly winding. Examination of the separations revealed evidence consistent with tensile overload.

Examination of the rudder control cable circuit and associated hardware did not reveal any evidence of a preexisting jam or failure. Flight control cable continuity for the rudder was established from the control surfaces to the cockpit controls. The stops for the rudder were examined; no evidence of severe repetitive strike marks or deformations was noted.

The electrically driven wing flap jackscrew actuator was not recovered. The flap switch in the cockpit was destroyed. The throttle and propeller controls were found in the FULL-FORWARD position. The mixture control was broken. The alternate air control was found in the CLOSED position. The key in the magneto switch was found in the BOTH position.

The tachometer needle was found intact, fixed in place, and pointed to 2,750 rpm. The red line on the tachometer began at 2,700 rpm. The hour register inside the tachometer read 0663.5 hours. The manifold pressure gauge needle was found fixed in place and indicated 27 inches Hg. The fuel flow gauge needle was found slightly loose and indicated 22 gallons per hour. The exhaust gas temperature gauge needle was found loose and indicated 1,000 degrees Fahrenheit (F). The oil temperature gauge was found fixed and indicated 150 degrees F. The oil pressure gauge was found fixed and indicated about 17 pounds per square inch (psi). The cylinder temperature gauge needle was not found. The fuel quantity gauges were destroyed. The altimeter needle was found fixed and indicated 270 feet. The altimeter setting was found fixed at 30.09 Hg. The top of the VOR indicator heading card was found at the 097-degree bearing.

Examination of all recovered electrical wiring and components did not reveal any evidence of arcing or fire. The circuit breaker panel was deformed and impact damaged. All of the breakers were found in the tripped position, except for the flap, transceiver, and DME. The circuit breaker that provided protection for the transponder, which provided the VFR code and altitude readout to radar facilities down to 1,100 feet, was also found tripped.

The fuel selector valve was recovered, and the bottom of the valve was missing. All three fuel line connections were broken off. The valve had separated from the fuselage attach points. The selector valve linkage was deformed, and the valve was found in the OFF position.

A liquid that had a similar color, odor, and texture as 100 low-lead aviation gasoline was found in the fuel selector valve sump. The electrically driven fuel boost pump was able to function when electrical power was applied to it.

The airplane had been equipped with six seats. The seats had been configured in a "club style" arrangement, with two forward-facing seats in row 1 (including the pilot's seat), two aft-facing seats in row 2, and two front-facing seats in row 3. The five recovered seats had separated from the floor structure. Examination of the aluminum backs of both aft-facing seats revealed that they were deformed (bulged) in the forward direction.

The left and right front seats were equipped with lap belts and shoulder harnesses. None of the belts for these seats could be identified in the wreckage. The four seats in rows 2 and 3 were also equipped with lap belts and shoulder harnesses. Both sections of the lap belt for the left-side aft-facing seat were found and exhibited evidence of stretching. The inboard section of the lap belt for the right-side aft-facing seat in row 2 had been cleanly cut about 3 inches from the male-end of the latch, and the outboard section of lap belt for this seat exhibited evidence of stretching. All of the lap belt sections for the seats in row 3 were identified and none exhibited evidence of stretching. The shoulder harnesses for the rear seats could not be identified in the wreckage.

MEDICAL AND PATHOLOGICAL INFORMATION

On July 21, 1999, examinations were performed on the pilot and passengers by Dr. James Weiner, Office of the Chief Medical Examiner, Commonwealth of Massachusetts. The results indicated that the pilot and passengers died from multiple injuries as a result of an airplane accident.

Toxicological testing was conducted by the FAA Toxicology Accident Research Laboratory, Oklahoma City, Oklahoma. The toxicological tests were negative for alcohol and drugs of abuse.

Medical Information

According to medical records, on June 1, 1999, the pilot fractured his left ankle in a "hang gliding" accident, and on June 2, 1999, he underwent surgical "open reduction internal fixation of left ankle fracture." On June 23, 1999, the pilot's leg was removed from a cast and placed in a "Cam-Walker." On July 15, 1999, the pilot's Cam-Walker was removed, and on July 16, 1999, he was given a "straight cane and instructed in cane usage." The medical records noted that the pilot was "full-weight bearing with mild antalgic gait."

During interviews, the pilot's physical therapist stated that the pilot did not have full dorsiflexion (bending upward of the foot) and that he could not determine whether the pilot's gait was caused by his slight limitation of motion or by mild pain. The pilot's orthopedic surgeon stated that he felt that, at the time of the accident, the pilot would have been able to apply the type of pressure with the left foot that would normally be required by emergency brake application with the right foot in an automobile.

According to 14 CFR Section 61.53, "Prohibition On Operations During Medical Deficiency," in operations that required a medical certificate, a person shall not act as a pilot-in-command while that person, "(1) Knows or has reason to know of any medical condition that would make the person unable to meet the requirements for the medical certificate necessary for the pilot operation."

According to an FAA medical doctor, a pilot with the type of ankle injury that the accident pilot had at the time of the accident would not normally be expected to visit and receive approval from an FAA Medical Examiner before resuming flying activities.

TESTS AND RESEARCH

Engine and Propeller Examinations

On July 26, 1999, the engine was examined at the Textron-Lycoming Facility, Williamsport, Pennsylvania, under the supervision of a Safety Board powerplants investigator. On July 28, 1999, the propeller hub and blades were examined at the Hartzell Propeller Facility, Piqua, Ohio, under the supervision of a Safety Board powerplants investigator. Parties to the investigation were present during both examinations.

According to the Powerplants Group Chairman's Factual Report, the examinations of the engine and propeller did not reveal evidence of any preexisting failures or conditions that would have prevented engine operation. The report further stated that "the investigation team found impact marks on one of the propeller blades and the top of the engine, witness marks inside the propeller, and the engine controls and instruments in the cockpit that indicated high engine power output."

Autopilot Operation

The airplane was equipped with a Bendix/King 150 Series Automatic Flight Control System (AFCS), which was approved for use in Piper PA-32R-301 model airplanes by the FAA on November 1, 1982.

The AFCS provided two-axis control for pitch and roll. It also had an electric pitch trim system, which provided autotrim during autopilot operation and manual electric trim for the pilot during manual operation.

The AFCS installed on the accident airplane had an altitude hold mode that, when selected, allowed the airplane to maintain the altitude that it had when the altitude hold was selected. The AFCS did not have the option of allowing the pilot to preselect an altitude so that the autopilot could fly to and maintain the preselected altitude as it climbed or descended from another altitude. The AFCS had a vertical trim rocker switch installed so that the pilot could change the airplane's pitch up or down without disconnecting the autopilot. The rocker switch allowed the pilot to make small corrections in the selected altitude while in the altitude hold mode or allowed the pitch attitude to be adjusted at a rate of about 0.9 degree per second when not in altitude hold mode.

The AFCS incorporated a flight director, which had to be activated before the autopilot would engage. Once activated, the flight director could provide commands to the flight command indicator to maintain wings level and the pitch attitude. To satisfy the command, the pilot could manually fly the airplane by referencing the guidance received in the flight command indicator, or the pilot could engage the autopilot and let it satisfy the commands by maneuvering the aircraft in a similar manner via the autopilot servos.

The AFCS incorporated a navigation mode that could provide guidance to the pilot, or the autopilot, about intercepting and tracking VOR and GPS courses. While engaged in this mode, the AFCS could receive input signals from either the selected VOR frequency and course or from GPS course data selected for presentation on the pictorial navigation indicator. The flight command indicator could then command the bank required to maintain the selected VOR or GPS course with automatic crosswind compensation, and the autopilot, if engaged, would satisfy those commands.

The AFCS incorporated a heading select mode that allowed the pilot to select a heading by moving a "bug" on the outer ring of the pictorial navigation indicator. Once the bug was moved to the desired heading with the heading select button engaged, the autopilot could command the airplane to that heading at a bank angle of about 22 degrees.

The AFCS had a control wheel steering (CWS) button mounted on the control yoke that allowed the pilot to maneuver the aircraft in pitch and roll without disengaging the autopilot. According to AlliedSignal, when the CWS button was released, the autopilot would resume control of the aircraft at the heading and altitude that had been selected at the time the CWS button was released.

According to the FAA and Bendix/King, the trim system was designed to withstand any single in-flight malfunction. Trim faults were visually and aurally annunciated in the cockpit. Through the use of monitor circuits, aircraft control would automatically be returned to the pilot when a fault was detected.

After the AFCS had been preflight tested, it could be engaged and disengaged either manually or automatically. The following conditions would cause the autopilot to automatically disengage: power failure, internal flight control system failure, loss of a valid compass signal, roll rates greater than 14 degrees per second, and pitch rates greater than 8 degrees per second.

Avionics Examinations

On July 29 and 30, 1999, the avionics were examined at the AlliedSignal/King Radios Facility, Olathe, Kansas, under the supervision of a Safety Board investigator. On October 13 and 14, 1999, a follow-up examination of the navigation and communications transceivers and all three autopilot servos was also performed at the AlliedSignal/King Radios Facility under the supervision of a Safety Board investigator. parties to the investigation were present during both examinations.

The accident airplane's AFCS was examined. Examination and functional testing of the AFCS pitch,

pitch trim, and roll servos did not reveal any evidence of a preimpact malfunction or jam.

The accident airplane was equipped with a GPS receiver, Bendix/King model KLN-90B. The GPS was capable of presenting moving map displays; bearings and distances to programmable destinations, such as airports and waypoints; airport information; ground speed; and other information. The GPS was also capable of interfacing with the AFCS and the pictorial navigation indicator.

Examination of the GPS unit revealed that it was crushed vertically. The display in the front face of the unit was destroyed. The ON/OFF switch was found in the ON position. The navigation database indicated that it was effective on October 8, 1998, and that it expired on November 4, 1998. A wire that connected the circuitry of a 3.6-volt lithium battery was separated. According to AlliedSignal, the lithium battery provided electrical power to retain the nonvolatile memory of the GPS receiver and required a minimum of 2.5 volts to retain memory. The battery voltage was measured to be 0.2 volt, and it was determined that the memory had not been retained.

Examination of the Bendix/King model KR-87, automatic direction finder, revealed that the receiver's primary frequency was set at 400 kilohertz (kHz) and the secondary frequency was set at 200 kHz.

Both of the airplane's communication/navigation transceivers received severe impact damage and could not be powered up. The nonvolatile memory circuit chips were extracted from the transceivers, placed in a test unit, and powered up. The following information was noted about each of the transceivers:

Transceiver No. 1, KX-165

The in-use communication frequency was set at 132.02, which was the same frequency as the TEB automatic terminal information service (ATIS).

The standby communication frequency was set at 135.25; the CDW ATIS had a frequency of 135.5.

The in-use navigation frequency was set at 109.80, which was the same frequency as the New Haven, Connecticut, VOR.

The standby navigation frequency was set at 113.10, which was the same frequency as the LaGuardia Airport, New York, VOR.

Transceiver No. 2, KX-165

The in-use communication frequency was set at 121.40, which was the same frequency as the MVY tower.

The standby communication frequency was set at 127.25; the MVY ATIS had a frequency of 126.25.

The in-use navigation frequency was set at 108.80, which was the same frequency as the BDR VOR.

The standby navigation frequency was set at 110.00, which was the same frequency as the Norwich, Connecticut, VOR.

Safety Board Materials Laboratory Examinations

An examination of the accident airplane's components was conducted in the Safety Board Materials Laboratory in Washington, D.C.

The flight command indicator (Bendix/King model KI-256) was deformed, and its glass faceplate was missing. The center portion of the pictorial display was partially embedded in the side of the housing in a position that indicated a right turn with a bank angle of about 125 degrees and a nose-down pitch attitude of about 30 degrees. The air-driven gyro housing inside of the flight command indicator was corroded but not deformed. Disassembly and inspection of the gyro did not reveal any scoring marks on the spinning mass gyro and mating housing. The turn coordinator was deformed, and its glass was missing. The display was captured in a position indicating a steep right turn. The electrically driven gyro assembly inside of the instrument was removed and found free to rotate with no binding or case interference. No scoring marks were found on either the spinning mass gyro or mating housing.

The pictorial navigation indicator (Bendix/King model KI-525A) was deformed, and its glass faceplate was missing. The heading indicator was pointing to 339 degrees. The center navigational display needle was oriented along the 300/120-degree bearing. The heading flag was displayed. The heading bug was located at the 095-degree mark. The slaved gyro assembly was partially separated from its mounting, and its case exhibited minor deformation. The gyro housing and internal rotor were disassembled. The interior surface of the case and the exterior surface of the spinning mass rotor did not exhibit any deformation, impact marks, or rotational scoring.

The engine-driven vacuum pump drive shear shaft was intact. The drive end was removed to expose the internal rotor and vanes. The rotor showed several cracks between the bottom of the vane slots and the center of the rotor. All six vanes were removed intact. The rotor was removed in several pieces, and the housing was examined. Examination revealed no evidence of scoring or rotational damage. A metal straight-edge was placed along the long ends of each vane, and no warping or wear was noted.

The electrically driven vacuum pump drive shear shaft was intact. The pump was opened from the motor drive end to expose the rotor and internal vanes. Several cracks were noted in the rotor between the vane slots and the center shaft area. Five of the six vanes were removed and found intact with no fractures or edge chipping. The sixth vane was found wedged and stuck in the rotor, which was stuck inside the housing. Approximately half of the rotor was removed, and examination of its housing revealed no evidence of scoring or rotational damage. A metal straight-edge was placed along the long ends of the removed vanes, and no warping or wear was noted. Disassembly and examination of the vacuum system filter did not reveal any evidence of contaminants or blockages.

The airspeed indicator was damaged, and its glass faceplate was missing. The needle position was found off-scale near the right edge of the density altitude adjustment window; it could be moved, however, when released, it spring-loaded to its as-found position. Magnified examination of marks on the instrument face revealed an outline similar to the size and shape of the needle. This mark was located about two needle widths above the 210-knot marking, which was the maximum marking on the indicator. The location of the needle mark on the airspeed indicator was consistent with the maximum mechanical needle travel position for the airspeed indicator design.

The VSI needle was missing. Magnified examination of marks on the instrument face revealed an outline similar to the size and shape of a needle. This needle mark was pointed at the down-limit position of 2,000 fpm descent.

Microscopic examination of the AFCS light bulbs on the front face of the unit was performed. None of the light bulbs exhibited evidence of filament stretch, including the autopilot engage, flight director, or trim failure light bulbs. An examination of all recovered light bulbs from the airplane's main and landing gear annunciator panels revealed no evidence of filament stretch.

Aircraft Performance Study

An aircraft performance study was performed by a Safety Board specialist using the Board's computer simulation program. According to the specialist's report, airplane performance data for the final portion of the flight were calculated using radar, aircraft, and weather data. Performance parameters were then computed for the final 7 minutes of the flight.

The calculated parameters showed the airplane initially descending from 5,500 feet at descent rates varying between 400 and 800 fpm, at 2133:40. At 2137:20, the airplane attained a steady descent rate of close to 600 fpm as the airplane passed through 3,000 feet. During the entire descent from 5,500 feet, the calculated airspeed remained near 160 KIAS, and the flightpath angle remained close to -2 degrees. About 2138, the airplane started to bank in a right-wing-down (RWD) direction toward a southerly direction. Calculated parameters indicated an almost constant roll angle of 13 degrees RWD and a vertical acceleration of 1.09 Gs while executing the turn. About 30 seconds after the turn was initiated, at an altitude of 2,200 feet, the airplane stopped descending. The airplane then climbed for the next 30 seconds, attaining a maximum climb rate of 600 fpm. During the ascent, the airplane finished the turn to a southeasterly direction, reduced speed slightly to 153 KIAS, and returned to a wings-level attitude by 2138:50. By 2139, the airplane leveled at 2,500 feet and then flew in a southeasterly direction with wings level while increasing airspeed back to 160 KIAS.

At 2139:50, the airplane entered a left turn, while slightly increasing altitude to 2,600 feet. The airplane reached a maximum bank angle of 28 degrees left-wing-down (LWD) and a maximum vertical acceleration of 1.2 Gs in this turn. When the maximum LWD bank angle was obtained, the altitude started to decrease at a descent rate close to 900 fpm. The LWD attitude was maintained for approximately 15 seconds until the airplane was heading towards the east. At 2140:07, the airplane bank angle returned to wings level. At 2140:15, with the airplane continuing towards the east, it reestablished a descent close to 900 fpm and then started to increase its bank angle in a RWD direction at nearly a constant rate. As the airplane bank angle increased, the rate of descent increased, and the airspeed started to increase. By 2140:25, the bank angle exceeded 45 degrees, the vertical acceleration was 1.2 Gs, the airspeed increased through 180 knots, and the flightpath angle was close to 5 degrees airplane nose down. After 2140:25, the airplane's airspeed, vertical acceleration, bank, and dive angle continued to increase, and the right turn tightened until water impact, about 2141.

ADDITIONAL INFORMATION

Cell Phones

The cell phone records for the three occupants of the airplane reflected one out-going call, about 2025. No calls were listed as being made from, or received by, the cell phones from the time of the takeoff through the estimated time of the accident.

Preflight Briefing

The AIM, published by the FAA, is the official guide to basic flight information and ATC procedures. Under the Section, "Preflight Briefing," it states that FSSs are the primary source for obtaining preflight briefings and in-flight weather information. The AIM states that a standard briefing should be requested any time a pilot is planning a flight and has not received a previous briefing or has not received preliminary information through mass dissemination media. The standard briefing should include the following information:

Adverse Conditions: Significant meteorological and aeronautical information that might influence the pilot to alter the proposed flight.

VFR Flight Not Recommended: When VFR flight is proposed and sky conditions or visibilities are present or forecast, surface or aloft, that in the briefer's judgment would make flight under VFR doubtful, the briefer will describe the conditions, affected locations, and use the phrase "VFR flight not recommended."

Current Conditions: Reported weather conditions applicable to the flight will be summarized from all available sources.

En Route Forecast: Forecast en route conditions for the proposed route are summarized in logical order (for example, departure/climbout, en route, and descent).

Destination Forecast: The destination forecast for the planned estimated time of arrival. Any significant changes within 1 hour before and after the planned arrival are included.

Winds Aloft: Forecast winds aloft will be provided using degrees of the compass. The briefer will interpolate wind directions and speeds between levels and stations as necessary to provide expected conditions at planned altitudes.

The AIM also states that a standard briefing should include synopsis, notices to airmen, and ATC delays.

Spatial Disorientation

A review of 14 CFR Part 61, "Certification: Pilots, Flight Instructors, and Ground Instructors," revealed that no specific training requirements exist regarding spatial disorientation. According to the FAA Practical

Test Standards, an applicant for a private pilot rating must exhibit knowledge of spatial disorientation. In addition, the publication states that "the examiner shall also emphasize stall/spin awareness, spatial disorientation..."

A review of training records from FSI revealed that while the pilot was preparing for his private pilot certificate, he received instruction on the symptoms, causes, and effects of spatial disorientation and the correct action to take if it occurred. In addition, the pilot received unusual attitude training while attending the private pilot and instrument training courses at FSI.

According to an FAA Instrument Flying Handbook, Advisory Circular 61-27C (AC) (Section II, "Instrument Flying: Coping with Illusions in Flight"), one purpose for instrument training and maintaining instrument proficiency is to prevent a pilot from being misled by several types of hazardous illusions that are peculiar to flight. The AC states that an illusion or false impression occurs when information provided by sensory organs is misinterpreted or inadequate and that many illusions in flight could be created by complex motions and certain visual scenes encountered under adverse weather conditions and at night. It also states that some illusions may lead to spatial disorientation or the inability to determine accurately the attitude or motion of the aircraft in relation to the earth's surface. The AC also states that spatial disorientation as a result of continued VFR flight into adverse weather conditions is regularly near the top of the cause/factor list in annual statistics on fatal aircraft accidents.

The AC further states that the most hazardous illusions that lead to spatial disorientation are created by information received from motion sensing systems, which are located in each inner ear. The AC also states that the sensory organs in these systems detect angular acceleration in the pitch, yaw, and roll axes, and a sensory organ detects gravity and linear acceleration and that, in flight, the motion sensing system may be stimulated by motion of the aircraft alone or in combination with head and body movement. The AC lists some of the major illusions leading to spatial disorientation as follows:

"The leans - A banked attitude, to the left for example, may be entered too slowly to set in motion the fluid in the 'roll' semicircular tubes. An abrupt correction of this attitude can now set the fluid in motion and so create the illusion of a banked attitude to the right. The disoriented pilot may make the error of rolling the aircraft back into the original left-banked attitude or, if level flight is maintained, will feel compelled to lean to the left until this illusion subsides.

Coriolis illusion - An abrupt head movement made during a prolonged constant-rate turn may set the fluid in more than one semicircular tube in motion, creating the strong illusion of turning or accelerating, in an entirely different axis. The disoriented pilot may maneuver the aircraft into a dangerous attitude in an attempt to correct this illusory movement...

Graveyard spiral - In a prolonged coordinated, constant-rate turn, the fluid in the semicircular tubes in the axis of the turn will cease its movement...An observed loss altitude in the aircraft instruments and the absence of any sensation of turning may create the illusion of being in a descent with the wings level. The disoriented pilot may pull back on the controls, tightening the spiral and increasing the loss of altitude...

Inversion illusion - An abrupt change from climb to straight-and-level flight can excessively stimulate the sensory organs for gravity and linear acceleration, creating the illusion of tumbling backwards. The disoriented pilot may push the aircraft abruptly into a nose-low attitude, possibly intensifying this illusion.

Elevator illusion - An abrupt upward vertical acceleration, as can occur in a helicopter or an updraft, can shift vision downwards (visual scene moves upwards) through excessive stimulation of the sensory organs for gravity and linear acceleration, creating the illusion of being in a climb. The disoriented pilot may push the aircraft into a nose low attitude. An abrupt downward vertical acceleration, usually in a downdraft, has the opposite effect, with the disoriented pilot pulling the aircraft into a nose-up attitude...

Autokinesis - In the dark, a stationary light will appear to move about when stared at for many seconds. The disoriented pilot could lose control of the aircraft in attempting to align it with the false movements of this light."

The AC also states that these undesirable sensations cannot be completely prevented but that they can be ignored or sufficiently suppressed by pilots' developing an "absolute" reliance upon what the flight instruments are reporting about the attitude of their aircraft. The AC further states that practice and experience in instrument flying are necessary to aid pilots in discounting or overcoming false sensations.

Further, the FAA Airplane Flying Handbook, FAA-H-8083-3, chapter 10, states the following about night flying and its affect on spatial orientation:

"Night flying requires that pilots be aware of, and operate within, their abilities and limitations. Although careful planning of any flight is essential, night flying demands more attention to the details of preflight preparation and planning. Preparation for a night flight should include a thorough review of the available weather reports and forecasts with particular attention given to temperature/dewpoint spread. A narrow temperature/dewpoint spread may indicate the possibility of ground fog. Emphasis should also be placed on wind direction and speed, since its effect on the airplane cannot be as easily detected at night as during the day...Night flying is very different from day flying and demands more attention of the pilot. The most noticeable difference is the limited availability of outside visual references. Therefore, flight instruments should be used to a greater degree in controlling the airplane...Under no circumstances should a VFR night-flight be made during poor or marginal weather conditions unless both the pilot and aircraft are certificated and equipped for flight under...IFR...Crossing large bodies of water at night in single-engine airplanes could be potentially hazardous, not only from the standpoint of landing (ditching) in the water, but also because with little or no lighting the horizon blends with the water, in which case, depth perception and orientation become difficult. During poor visibility conditions over water, the horizon will become obscure, and may result in a loss of orientation. Even on clear nights, the stars may be reflected on the water surface, which could appear as a continuous array of lights, thus making the horizon difficult to identify."

According to AC 60-4A, "Pilot's Spatial Disorientation," tests conducted with qualified instrument pilots indicated that it can take as long as 35 seconds to establish full control by instruments after a loss of visual reference of the earth's surface. AC 60-4A further states that surface references and the natural horizon may become obscured even though visibility may be above VFR minimums and that an inability to perceive the natural horizon or surface references is common during flights over water, at night, in sparsely populated areas, and in low-visibility conditions.

A book titled, Night Flying, by Richard Haines and Courtney Flatau, provides some additional information concerning vertigo and disorientation. It states the following:

"Vestibular disorientation refers to the general feeling that one's flight path isn't correct in some way. By calling this effect vestibular, it emphasizes the role played by the middle ear's balance organ. Flying an uncoordinated turn produces this effect as does excessive head turning during a turn in flight. Vestibular disorientation is often subtle in its onset, yet it is the most disabling and dangerous of all disorientation."

Pilot's Operating Handbook (POH)

According to the POH and a photo of the accident airplane's cockpit, the fuel selector control was located below the center of the instrument panel, on the sloping face of the control tunnel, on the cockpit floor. In the "Normal Procedures" section of the POH, under "Cruising," it states, "In order to keep the airplane in best lateral trim during cruise flight, the fuel should be used alternately from each tank at one hour intervals." Also, in the "Normal Procedures" section, under the "Approach and Landing" checklist, the first item listed is "Fuel selector - proper tank."

Wreckage Release

On August 5, 1999, the main airplane wreckage was released to a representative of the accident pilot's insurance company. On November 17, 1999, the remainder of the retained parts were released and shipped to the insurance company's storage facility.

Additional Persons Participating in the Investigation:

Richard I. Bunker - Massachusetts Aeronautics Commission, Boston, Massachusetts

Tom McCreary - Hartzell Propeller Inc., Piqua, Ohio

Albert Pecker

Sectional Maps of JFK Jr.'s Route

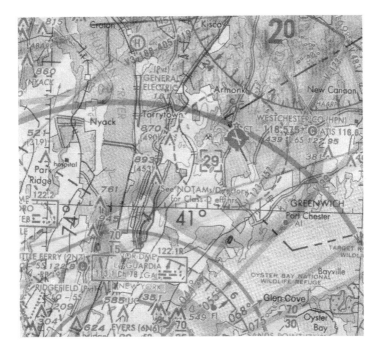

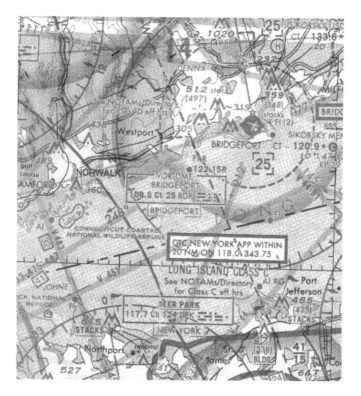

Albert Pecker

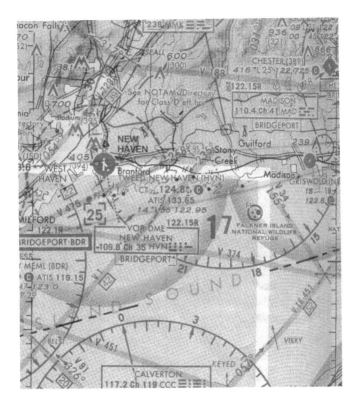

156

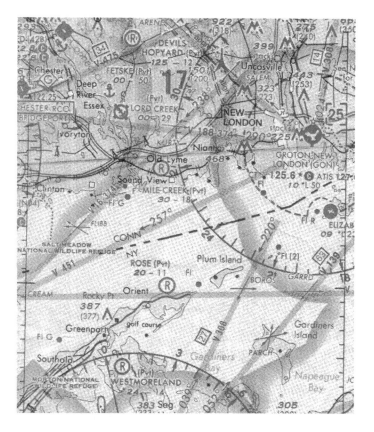

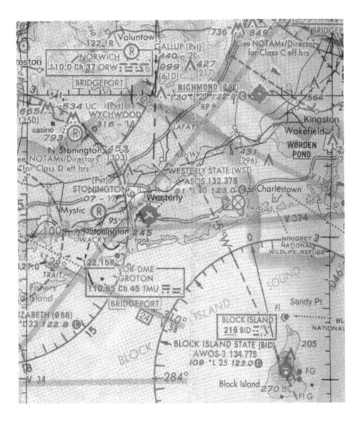

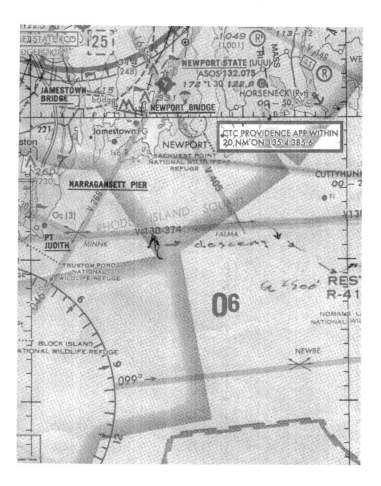

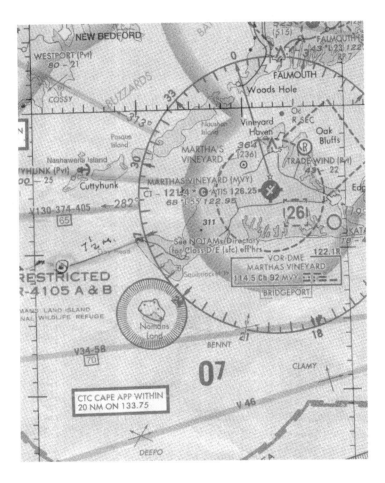

ABOUT THE AUTHOR

Albert Pecker has been flying for more than 20 years, and has loved every knee knocking minute of it. Laid up after a leg injury, he decided to write about his most frightening flying mishaps, prompted by a friends questions about JFK Jr.'s fatal crash, in a plane like one he himself flew. Albert was born in Brooklyn, N.Y., 1931, in the Flatbush section of Brooklyn, attended Stuyvesant High School in Manhattan, and went on to City College school of Engineering at Convent Ave and 137th St Manhattan (tuition $12.00/semester). Drafted into the U.S. army during the Korean War, he then worked as a structural engineer and builder in New Jersey.